T0247713

PRAISE FOR *NEVER LEAD ALONE*

"Today's dynamic world requires a richness of insight best achieved through teamship. . . . *Never Lead Alone* reveals the practices for breakthrough performance of any modern team."
    —*Bejul Somaia, global partner, Lightspeed*

"Ferrazzi's continued focus on simple-to-execute teamship processes will enable organizations to truly thrive!"
    —*Paul Bay, CEO, Ingram Micro*

"*Never Lead Alone* concepts and practical tools are critical components to win in today's marketplace and create step-change outcomes."
    —*Deepa Soni, CIO and COO, Hartford Financial Services Group*

"A fresh perspective on how collaborative engagement and problem-solving can radically accelerate team performance."
    —*Keith Rick McConnell, CEO, Dynatrace*

"These insights are invaluable for all leaders striving to stay ahead of the curve."
    —*Bob Carrigan, CEO, Audible*

"*Never Lead Alone* sets the standard for being a high-impact, high-performing teammate on an elite team."
    —*Ana White, chief people officer, Lumen Technologies*

"A must-read for anyone who wants to elevate their professional and personal relationships through better collaboration and stronger teamwork."
    —*Jamie Iannone, CEO, eBay*

"An indispensable guide for all team members."
    —*Bob Toohey, EVP and CHRO, Allstate*

"Ferrazzi's playbook embodies so much of what we value at Mastercard—the ability to grow together, collaborate, and bring in diverse perspectives to unlock innovation."

—*Michael Fraccaro, chief people officer, Mastercard*

"Ferrazzi does a masterful job providing teams with a playbook to effectively collaborate, build trust, and promote inclusion to achieve extraordinary results."

—*Colin Walsh, CEO and cofounder, Varo Money*

" 'Teamship' will be the new terminology and practice that takes companies to the next level."

—*Scott Salmirs, CEO, ABM Industries*

"Ferrazzi brilliantly captures the essence of hyper-accountable, modern collaboration."

—*Sean Behr, CEO, Fountain*

"The world needs a practical (not theoretical) road map for how we build extraordinary teams. This book is exactly that."

—*Ed McLaughlin, president and CTO, Mastercard*

"Ferrazzi has a distinctive gift for bringing people together to have deeply meaningful conversations. . . . He brings this perspective to the concept of teamship."

—*Lucien Alziari, EVP and CHRO, Prudential Financial*

"These principles are challenging, sharp, and key to accelerating deeply connected teams that produce high-performance outcomes."

—*Shane Grant, group deputy CEO, Danone*

"Ferrazzi delivers a new take on teams that is really needed. I hope it is read widely."

—*Bracken Darrell, CEO, VF Corporation*

NEVER LEAD
ALONE

Also by Keith Ferrazzi

Never Eat Alone

Who's Got Your Back

Leading Without Authority

Competing in the New World of Work

NEVER LEAD ALONE

10 SHIFTS FROM LEADERSHIP TO *TEAMSHIP*

KEITH FERRAZZI

WITH PAUL HILL

HARPER
BUSINESS

An Imprint of HarperCollinsPublishers

HarperCollins books may be purchased for educational, business, or sales promotional use. For information, please email the Special Markets Department at SPsales@harpercollins.com.

FIRST EDITION

Library of Congress Cataloging-in-Publication Data
Names: Ferrazzi, Keith, author. | Hill, Paul, author.
Title: Never lead alone: 10 shifts from leadership to teamship / Keith Ferrazzi, with Paul Hill.
Description: First edition. | New York, NY : Harper Business, [2024] | Includes bibliographical references.
Identifiers: LCCN 2024028296 (print) | LCCN 2024028297 (ebook) | ISBN 9780063412576 (hardcover) | ISBN 9780063412569 (ebook)
Subjects: LCSH: Teams in the workplace. | Leadership.
Classification: LCC HD66 .F475 2024 (print) | LCC HD66 (ebook) | DDC 658.4/022—dc23/eng/20250620
LC record available at https://lccn.loc.gov/2024028296
LC ebook record available at https://lccn.loc.gov/2024028297

ISBN 978-0-06-341257-6

24 25 26 27 28 LBC 5 4 3 2 1

This book is dedicated to Kale,
my ultimate Co-elevation partner.

CONTENTS

CONTENTS

CHAPTER I

CRACKING THE CODE OF TEAMSHIP

TEAMSHIP:
The ultimate competitive advantage driven by:

(A) shifting from traditional hierarchies to teammates co-leading teams and elevating each other to achieve world-class performance; and

(B) shifting from standard working habits to inclusive twenty-first-century collaboration practices, processes, and tools to achieve bolder innovation and faster decision-making.

When I wrote my first book, *Never Eat Alone*, with Tahl Raz, I didn't imagine how much it would change the trajectory of how people thought about relationships and networking from something transactional to an authentic investment in a real relationship that starts with generosity: really busting your back end to be of service to others. The meaningful lesson was whatever you want out of your life, the mission you want to achieve, the prosperity that you hope for yourself, for your family, for your community, for your cause, there are a handful of people critical to strapping a booster rocket on every dream you've ever had. You open these doors with beautiful generosity and authenticity so that these relationships flourish. It's so simple, so powerful, such a joyful way to live, and it's what I've built my success and life upon. But I never saw networking as my life's purpose. For years, and despite its success, I almost turned my back on *Never Eat Alone*. I had people from all around the world come up to me saying that the book changed their life. I felt blessed, but I didn't really internalize that because I was aiming at something very different: a purpose I've felt since I was a scrappy poor kid growing up in Latrobe, Pennsylvania, watching my dad, an unemployed steelworker, taking any job to get some money coming in—digging ditches—and my mom on her knees scrubbing floors for twenty bucks a day. You can see that purpose running through all of my books and right back to my childhood—the desire to figure out how to help people through transforming business, to get under the hood of how to make organizations better, for folks like my dad and families like ours who had suffered, but also for the elevation of communities. To transform teams to transform the world. I want to crack the code—I am a behavioral engineer focused on high-return practices. That's what *Never Lead Alone* is about. The world needs a practical (not theoretical) roadmap for how we build extraordinary teams. What it means to be an extraordinary teammate and what practices all of us can integrate into our work and coach into others around us. This book, my life's work, is that practice-based roadmap. We can all achieve disproportionately extraordinary things with a strong team of committed souls around us, and learning that started way back home in Latrobe. And the irony in having turned my attention away from being the "networking guy"? Twenty years after *Never Eat Alone* was published, I appreciate and embrace a throughline in all my research and writing: that work today happens fluidly in networked teams, and the productivity of teams is powered by purposefully engineered relationships.

GOING BACK TO THE SOURCE

My old man was an unemployed steelworker whose family emigrated from Italy to find prosperity and ended up a victim of the steel industry crash that hit Pittsburgh, Pennsylvania, and all across the Rust Belt in the 1970s. As a kid, I would hear my father come home and bemoan at the dinner table about the practices that were going on in his workplace. His manager would literally tell him to slow down because he was making the boss look bad as he was outworking his peers and throwing off the measured piece rate by his work pace. If you look back at the newspaper headlines in the seventies, you would have seen stories about "cheap foreign imports from Japan," and the accusation was that Japanese labor was flooding the American marketplace, allowing inappropriate competition. But really, something else was going on.

Total Quality Management (TQM) was created by academics in the United States to expect more from frontline teams; men like my father would work to drive outrageous results like zero defects through empowered teams. But this new way of working was ignored by the arrogant steel industry, despite being adopted in Japanese factories to deliver less-expensive and higher-quality products. I would study this in college, and it would become another formative thread in my belief that transforming teams really can transform organizations. But as a kid, I'm sitting there hearing my dad lament everything that we were suffering. He was now unemployed, striving to make ends meet, taking any job possible. My mom had to go get a job as a cleaning lady, which she hated. But what was most important was at the age of ten, I committed to my dad that someday, I would grow up (now you're going to laugh) to be governor of Pennsylvania and then president of the United States, and I would fix American manufacturing. What did I know? Everyone we knew was a blue-collar working family. I just reached as high as I could imagine to be in a position to change the economic state of families like ours.

If you've read *Never Eat Alone*, you'll know that I ended up on my way to Yale with the help of a number of amazing benefactors. There's no nepotism when you grow up in a family where no one went to college—unless you "create your own nepotism" through the caring network you nurture yourself. It's the same principle I'd coach years later in the book *Leading Without Authority*: how leaders working outside the authority they may possess according to the org chart could achieve extraordinary things working across silos. But at Yale I did run for political office, for city council in New Haven, Connecticut. The story picked up coverage in the *New York Times*, and people started calling me from back in Pennsylvania, wealthy individuals, to say, "Come back when you're done with Yale. We want you to run." So I did. When I left Yale, I did two things. While the prize job of the eighties was Wall Street, I was the only Yale grad to go to work in manufacturing as a leader in Total Quality Management for a chemical company that sold into General Motors. I also found a congressional district I thought I could win.

But something happened that threw a curveball at me. I fell in love with a fraternity brother. I bet you didn't see that coming, and neither did I as a Christian from blue-collar Pennsylvania. And that was the end of my political aspirations. Back in those days, even Liberace was straight. I joke, but it was a gut-wrenching, existential reconciliation at the time. There were literally no role models, and I didn't have the courage to be the first.

But I saw a pivot.

I was already doing impactful work down on the plant floor. I could double down and materialize my mission to save American manufacturing another way. Maybe I could do it through the American corporation itself, by working in business? And maybe I could be authentic to myself outside the public eye of politics. So I went to Harvard Business School. And, who funded my tuition? My mentors and benefactors who were prepared to invest in my congressional election. The people whom you robustly serve as an authentic human, they will be there for you as you invite them to new and evolving co-creations. You will see that foundation stone of relationships throughout this book and your life.

EXPERIENCING TEAMS AT DELOITTE AND STARWOOD

From Harvard, I joined Deloitte, where I became the youngest person to be elected partner and the global CMO at lightning speed, which was actually why I was asked to write *Never Eat Alone*, a story of how to radically accelerate success through better relationship management. I started Deloitte research to develop new methodologies for transforming work, beyond TQM, and adopted mentors like Michael Hammer to create our practice of reengineering and change management, which helped me refine my taste for cracking the code of ways of working. I also teamed up with a group of executives in Chicago to found the Lincoln Foundation for Business Excellence to create an award to recognize and guide organizations in adopting effective new ways of working. Ultimately, excited to put these ideas into action, I left to join Starwood Hotels as CMO and head of global sales. I quickly realized that things were different. At Deloitte, we were a team taking a hill together. Our goal was to be at par someday with Accenture and McKinsey, but we were the lowest of the Big Eight global consultancies in brand recognition and other metrics. Despite that, we were a strong team on a shared mission. When I left to join Starwood, we had a similar aspiration to reinvent the hospitality industry but were not a cohesive team. Starwood had four CEOs over five years and despite great innovations like our award-winning SPG loyalty program, the W Hotel, and the design of the pillow-topped mattress, the "Heavenly Bed," we were subscale compared to our big competitors Hilton and Marriott, and the costs Starwood allocated per hotel (for global sales and call centers, for example) were much higher. Individual teammates had all the insight we needed; we had strong hotel operators, brilliant real estate and financial engineers, and breakthrough creative and marketing minds, but we never achieved the psychological safety and interdependency to bring it all together to win. Starwood sold to Marriott in 2016, not because it was doing great business, but because there was still some value left in our guest loyalty program. It wasn't a way to secure a great multiple. I saw so personally and intimately the power of what I now call teamship, and the experience was so eloquent—so rich at Deloitte, so raw at Starwood—I committed to founding my own research institute and coaching firm to inquire into and explore the practices of teamship.

TWO INFLUENCES

At that time, in the early 2000s, there were two strong influences on my thinking. One was the seminal work of Patrick Lencioni and his great book on the *Five Dysfunctions of a Team*. The other was Gallup's research on measuring employee engagement and correlating it to corporate performance. Gallup's breakthrough Q12 methodology was a powerful awakening for HR that culture could have directional metrics for business improvement. What I recognized was that this qualitative survey-based research had an individual-employee and enterprise focus but not a team orientation, which is what I was coming to believe is the essence of where and how work happens and can be most improved. It was certainly revelatory information at the time to understand that if an employee has a best friend at work (one of the early Gallup Q12) they would see an increase in engagement. And yet, it's a different and equally important vantage point to ask the question if the employee feels that their team has their back. As a leader or a teammate, I want to have a dashboard for the sentiment and performance of my teammates and clear practices to elevate us. We often go so quickly from looking at the individual and the leader to then aggregating up to the enterprise that we miss the critical analysis and intervention of the team. I wanted to see a dashboard showing how our teams are doing and compare them to high-performing teams within and elsewhere. I approached one of the leaders of Gallup at the time, who had been instrumental in developing and researching employee engagement, and suggested we create the most rigorous possible team performance diagnostic. And we did. This is a major missing piece of most leaders' and teams' performance dashboard. You'll read about the diagnostic in chapter 2 and experience it in the pages that follow. That was the genesis of the Greenlight Research Institute, an applied research body dedicated to designing practical interventions, which we call high-return teamship practices. We draw together primary research from the likes of Oxford, Wharton, the Massachusetts Institute of Technology (MIT), and Harvard Business School, matched with real-world observations over twenty years of "laboratory" experience of coaching the world's top teams. I know that *Never Eat Alone* was such a sensation because it was so chock-full of simple practices that, if tried, could be game-changing. This book follows the same formula: there are more than thirty teamship practices to try.

INTRODUCING TEAMSHIP

For decades the role of the leader was elevated. But the world's best teams don't win because of leadership alone. They win largely because of their teamship. A good leader gives feedback. A great leader assures the team gives each other feedback. A good leader holds members of the team accountable; a great leader assures the team holds each other accountable. A good leader keeps the energy of the team strong; a great leader assures the team is responsible for each other's energy. But more than the leader, it's the responsibility of the team itself. Drop the leader from the prior comments and a great team gives each other feedback. A great team holds each other accountable. A great team is responsible for each other's energy. We will explore the data behind that analysis—the three thousand diagnostic assessments conducted with teams over twenty years of coaching—throughout this book.

WHY TEAMSHIP MATTERS

We expect everything of the leader and give too little focus to the teammates and their responsibility to each other. We've all but ignored how to extract billions of dollars of shareholder value from the interdependency of talent in and among teams. When we refer to a team, we don't just refer to the org chart, we mean the group working to achieve what needs to get done. Work happens in networks of teams. Upgrading teams and what it means to be a great teammate is one of the least-curated and underleveraged opportunities for accelerating business outcomes today. In fact, our research has uncovered that some of the greatest erosion of shareholder value comes from one single debilitating habit of most teammates: conflict avoidance. Teamship and our practices address that.

We have grown an elevated respect and admiration for the

image of a great leader. Yet, large companies and titans find themselves disrupted and toppled by start-ups with founder teams that have teamship born into their everyday behaviors and practices who commit to the mission and to each other. They are the lion's share of the top disruptive 15 percent of the teams discovered by our research, something we will begin to explore more in the next chapter. There is too little discussion about how a leader can encourage and shift teams from these all-too-present old behaviors to the world-class behaviors, processes, practices, and tools of teamship that the world of work demands today.

Teamship is engineered for today's volatile world. The volatility and performance pressure in the world around us call for extreme and collective purposefulness of teammates. We should have no time for frozen routines and ossified protocols that pose obstacles to growth. In my last book, *Competing in the New World of Work*, I described a methodology called radical adaptability, based on interviews and observations with more than two thousand leaders about accelerating change through uncertainty. Radical adaptability calls for a culture rooted in foresight, inclusion, agility, and resilience and the team behaviors and practices that will drive that. The aim is a working culture of agile and bold innovation and broader co-creation that happens in an accelerated way. The 10 shifts that are required to build teamship reflect today's world of hybrid work with networked teams. They speak to the need for a changing work contract and agility in a radically changing environment. They address issues that simply did not have the same place on the agenda two decades ago, like diversity, equity, and inclusion, or the emergence of artificial intelligence and its potential to transform team collaboration. To transform business outcomes in today's world, a new working culture needs to be forged into being.

THE TEAMSHIP FRAMEWORK

Ultimately, the shift to teamship has two driving forces:

1. **Co-elevating behaviors.** Co-elevation is the agreement among teammates that we coach teams to achieve. Co-elevation is the contract of a group of people deeply committed to achieving a mission, but also deeply committed to lifting each other up while achieving that mission. That means that teammates will not withhold the truth, we will not be conflict-avoidant, and we will share what we're feeling with each other. In our coaching we join the staff meetings and help a team to realize that even though there may be different disciplines or divisions represented in the room, they all need to share the same enterprise goal. It will free up 30 percent of a leader's time to have the team step up. And in addition, commiting to a team of co-elevating peers in the room will allow you to accelerate innovation, boldness, and extraordinary outcomes. We will learn more about awakening to Co-elevating behaviors in chapter 2.

2. **Twenty-first-century collaborative processes and tools.** This means no longer relying on old-school, ineffective meetings as the primary form of collaboration by (a) adopting asynchronous working patterns and collaboration software to shift whole cycles of collaboration ahead of meetings; (b) fostering more inclusive collaboration by again leveraging software to involve more people in co-creation to achieve bolder thinking without slowing things down; (c) adopting agile as an enterprise-wide operating system, not just in engineering or project management but from the C-suite team down; (d) thinking about how AI becomes part of the team. We will talk more about collaborative process, software, AI, and enterprise agile in chapters 6 and 7.

We can break down the big shift to teamship into 10 behaviorial and process shifts and simple practices that increasingly move from traditional command-and-control leadership to peers co-leading the team. This kind of leadership is seldom taught, as it's not the traditional leader-led model that we have all grown to expect.

Let's look at each shift in a little more detail:

1. Shifting from hub-and-spoke to the leader to Co-elevation of the team

The first shift is awakening team members to the hope and possibility of a new way of being and a heightened level of performance. We introduce the diagnostic exercise that starts to reveal the team's current state and gives them their first glimpse of how things could be if they choose to agree to a new social contract, to try on a different set of behaviors among them. This is the aha moment, reinforced by repeated application of new practices, which helps a team realize that something quite different is possible. The diagnostic features throughout the book.

2. Shifting from conflict avoidance to candor

There are no back-channel conversations in world-class teams, no critical direct messages between teammates about one another. Teammates have shifted to an agreement to care enough about each other's success that nothing will be withheld from each other or the team that might be valuable to achieving better outcomes.

3. Shifting from serendipitous relationships to purposeful team bond-building

Here we shift from accidental or serendipitous relationships at the proverbial watercooler to very purposeful bond-building that engineers trust and true understanding among peers. Teams that have shifted to purposeful bonding, especially those who are hybrid, have reaped high cultural rewards well above relying on the old walk down the hallway.

4. Shifting from individual to team resilience

This shift is for the team to accept the job of owning and lifting up each other's energy and sustaining team resilience. Having each other's back. Where do we turn when we hit a wall? Taking notice and responsibility for our energy levels can't just be our lone responsibility or even the job of the leader or HR anymore, it's our job as teammates.

5. Shifting to elevate collaboration: broader co-creation, and the adoption of meeting shifting

    Holding a meeting isn't the only form of collaboration—meetings are not even the first form of collaboration. We must shift to a bolder and more inclusive approach to collaboration that leads to a greater diversity of thinking and more innovative ideas from a broader network of stakeholders—inside and outside the organization. Ultimately, world-class teams think of collaboration not as a meeting but as a Collaboration Stack—a series of different modes of collaboration, from asynchronous to in-person, each of which must be purposefully engineered for. Even fully remote teams realize the importance of regular in-person engagement. Collaboration today must also include the introduction of new teamship processes and tools and the regular leverage of software, incorporating the perspectives of both human and AI teammates.

6. Shifting to executive and Team Agile

    The simple but powerful shift to an agile team process is the only viable operating system to navigate today's volatility and allow us to constantly look around corners and adapt to and accelerate the achievement of bold initiatives.

7. Shifting from a culture of leader-led praise to peer celebration and recognition

   For all the tough conversations and peer-to-peer accountability involved in teamship, we cannot forget the power of recognition and celebration, and like all other shifts, we can have it in abundance if it is engineered to come from our peers and not just our boss. Recognition and celebration keep driving us forward in the face of unprecedented obstacles and it's needed often, and from all around us.

8. Shifting to diversity, inclusion, and belonging

   If you had a team to coach for six months to become the shining emblem of diversity, equity, and inclusion, what would you do? This was the question I asked leaders at a World Economic Forum meeting in 2023. The most innovative teams relish and build greatness out of diverse perspectives. Turning what are often the unspoken and sensitive divides of otherness and privilege into bonding and productive conversations can have a massive impact on a team's ability to leverage the whole potential of the team for breakthrough innovation.

9. Shifting to a team of seekers who are each other's coaches

   In a world-class team, we are all constantly seeking growth, and this shift is from expecting the leader to be our coach to accepting our teammates as our coaches and holding each other accountable for our performance and growth.

10. Shifting from silos to alignment

When teams adopt the 10 shifts, they achieve what most fail to achieve and sustain: true and constant alignment even through all the twists and turns of a volatile world and becoming a radically adaptable team. But this is not about shifting mindsets alone. Shifting from old behaviors to Co-elevating behaviors along with the processes and tools of teamship turns our high-return practices into everyday team habits. One of my favorite sayings is, "We don't think our way into new ways of acting, we act our way into new ways of thinking." It's true.

At each stage of the transformation journey to teamship—as psychological safety grows, bold innovation accelerates, and breakthrough results follow—a suite of teamship practices turn the behaviors into reflexes: team habits.

INTRODUCING TEAMSHIP PRACTICES

Through our research and monitoring of thousands of teams, when we see what one might consider a "best practice" we take it out, refine it with secondary research, and reapply it to other teams in our research set until we know it will measurably move the needle. It then becomes a high-return teamship practice and we coach it into the teams we work with. Teamship practices are the easiest way to get your team to adopt a new behavior, and eventually a new mindset. A typical teamship practice is a simple, targeted task that is relatively easy to implement and, if repeated, will dramatically increase a team's effectiveness. Each chapter contains several practices that are designed to achieve behavioral change, improve team functioning, and improve the health of the overall organization. These practices have been the differentiating value of our team coaching for years—changing the culture of organizations through the practices and work of their teams. They have allowed us to scale our coaching beyond just me and to easily hire many coaches who are able to help teams bring these high-return teamship practices to life through repeated use over a six-month period. Coaches and teammates alike can become coaches of teamship in their work. It was this awareness that my own coaching could be scaled, and my desire to have a greater impact on the world of business and society, that made me decide to publish these practices and give all of you the same access as my coaches and clients have had to these shifts and practices. In your hands, you and your teammates can use Co-elevating behaviors, processes, and tools and move to teamship. The best next step is to nominate a teamship ambassador on the team who is passionate for the change and will assure everyone gives all the shifts and practices a healthy shot of adoption. In time, we all will become teamship ambassadors, but for starters, when the rest of us are quick to forget and fall back on old habits, having one ambassador with the leader and the team will help coach the new behaviors into play.

OUR JOURNEY TO TEAMSHIP

For the last twenty years, I've been coaching teams through the 10 shifts in six months with transformational results. Ideally, you are going to work through this book as a team, learning new behaviors and high-return practices together, trying them on iteratively. Throughout the book, you will be given a set of diagnostic questions that will help your team understand the difference between their current behaviors and practices and what's possible for a world-class team on a teamship journey. Use this book as a workbook as you move through the shift in each chapter and its associated teamship practices. You will be surprised how adopting the high-return practices will quickly bring out the realization of how far your team still needs to go. Trust the practices. Adopt them and use them to shift to being a dream team.

CHAPTER 2

SHIFTING FROM HUB-AND-SPOKE TO THE LEADER TO CO-ELEVATION OF THE TEAM

Red Flag Rule:
We are equally committed to all goals of the team and each other to get there.

---

ergey Young was doing what most leaders think is impossible: chasing down a moonshot 10x growth goal while freeing up 30 percent of his time. The team at his venture capital business was on an ambitious mission to increase assets under management tenfold to $10 billion while he was also looking to spend more time than ever on his real calling, the birth of a new fund and deep passion to prolong human life. Young is ex-McKinsey. Smart. Charming. Relentless in his drive, exacting in his standards. But to achieve what he wanted, Young needed to overcome the one big obstacle to his goals. His team needed to become the growth engine for his traditional VC business. Young's traditional behavior—his brilliance, appetite for work, and perfectionism—was limiting his ambition and his team's progress. He needed to share the load of leadership with his team.

Young's awakening happened in Rome, in the beautiful gardens of the Vatican City, sitting by a Renaissance fountain. We were both invited to a meeting hosted by the Pope and his council to explore the impacts on society of radically prolonging human life. Young was hungry to commit more time to an extraordinary mission to extend the healthy human lifespan by investing in longevity technologies and biotech via a new Longevity Vision Fund. Young is one of the co-creators of the XPRIZE Healthspan competition, which will award $101 million to any team that can, essentially, make humans ages 65+ at least two decades younger after only one year of treatment. It's a mission to democratize longevity; to extend the lifespan of all humans, not just the billionaire elite. Personally, Young hopes to live well beyond the age of one hundred with a body as fit and healthy as a twenty-five-year-old. You would not bet against him. But that day, talking in the tranquil Vatican gardens, I asked him: "What's your moonshot, Sergey? Is it shared by your teammates and are they able to get there?" He talked about his deep commitment to growth for his investors and the hope of freeing more of his time for his human longevity work. He thought of it as sequential, but I asked him, what if they were able to be achieved in parallel? If we could crack his hub-and-spoke leadership style, both goals would be within reach. Young had made his overcrowded schedule work by spending as little time as possible per task and directing individuals, rather than empowering the team of exceptionally smart people he had hired. If Young wanted to make that moonshot a reality, he would need to shift from reliance on his leadership to enabling teamship. As we explained in chapter 1, teamship is the way we see world-class teams win and it is the result of a simple equation: the adoption of what this chapter will define as Co-elevating behaviors among the teammates along with new collaborative processes, practices, and tools, detailed in the following chapters.

A few weeks later, I met Young and his senior team in a very different setting, on the top floor of a hotel in Las Vegas, for a coaching session. Looking back, Young says:

> With the team it was always, I give you a directive, you go and do it. It seemed to be the most efficient way to run the organization. Of course, I came to realize the problem was that my organization was too centered around me. I reached the limit of my—and therefore our—ability to grow. This realization was so clear that unless I changed the modus operandi for the team, and the way we work, we were going to be stuck at a pretty low level.

He used an elegant phrase to sum it up: he knew he had hired stars; now he needed a constellation. The question was, how to bring about such a shift?

INTRODUCING THE FIRST SHIFT: CO-ELEVATION

The first shift is an awakening and commitment to what we call Co-elevation behaviors—a big aha moment of realization about the mediocrity of how most of us have been working. Too many teammates operate in coexistence. They do their jobs and don't want to bother each other. They think it's their responsibility to get as much done in their silo as they can, and only accept collaboration when absolutely necessary—not because they think it will add richness to the answer, but because they are blocked. In the worst case, when collaboration is messy and disagreements occur and the relationships are weak, we slip into resentment between critical players who should be on the same team. But in most cases, we just miss the amazing opportunity to collaborate and push each other higher and achieve much more as a team than we could have individually. In a world of scarce resources and massive volatility, going at it alone is no solution for success, let alone exponential success. Most teams work like this; most leaders accept it, some even encourage it.

The alternative is Co-elevation. It is the driving set of behaviors behind teamship. Co-elevation is the set of behavioral commitments among a team to the mission and to each other, an unwavering belief in winning together and pushing each other higher in the process. Co-elevation behaviors and practices, coupled with teamship processes and tools, will get us to places we have only dreamed of. But that begins with recognizing that old-fashioned collaboration and assumptions of how we behave with each other and who we are as teammates need to have a seismic shift.

Fueled by this shift, the highest-performing teams can find unexpected growth and decrease unsuspected risk. They fight united to achieve audacious goals and find huge value among the interdependencies between them. Even when a team may be made up of very distinct divisions, teammates can awaken to the realization of the wisdom and insight that is pent up among their peers. I've witnessed this behavioral commitment executed in the very best of Fortune 500 companies, entrepreneurial mid-market brands, fast-growing start-ups, nongovernmental organizations (NGOs), and even governments we've worked with. These shifts and practices can work in a local restaurant as well! My favorite local restaurant, WeHo Bistro, applied the commitment to Co-elevation and now the owner has freed up 50 percent of his time and the food and quality of service and customer loyalty are off the charts. I wrote a piece about how the US government and cabinet could function better with Co-elevation and then went on to coach it into the government of Bhutan. I've seen Co-elevating teams create billions of dollars of shareholder value through innovation, transformation, and a stubborn refusal to let each other fail. They share the load of leadership to achieve extraordinary results. This is the shift that Sergey Young and his team needed.

My dear friend Peter Diamandis, cofounder of Singularity University, described the before and aftereffects of shifting to Co-elevation behaviors with his team at the XPRIZE Foundation. "At the end of the day, if you're feeling like you are responsible for everything and making sure everybody is doing everything all the time, it can get exhausting," Peter says. "After a commitment to Co-elevation, I am super proud of my team. And I feel a sense of being excited about the unexpected because I am not managing everything all the time. Amazing, surprising things can happen." In Co-elevating teams, close co-creative relationships are forged based on candid feedback and mutual accountability. The resulting outcomes almost always exceed what could have been accomplished through regular channels within the org chart. When we commit to teamship and the Co-elevation behaviors, we work with more positive energy, generate bolder innovative ideas, expand our abilities, and execute faster. Versus typical teams, our research shows Co-elevating teams gain a 79 percent increase in candor, a 46 percent increase in collaboration, and a 44 percent increase in accountability. Unfortunately, this is a standard of teamship that only 15 percent of the world's teams attain today.

TEAMSHIP PRACTICE: RECONTRACTING AND THE NEW SOCIAL CONTRACT FOR TEAMS

In addition to talking about an organization's "culture," I like to draw very clear and practical attention to a working team's "social contract." In fact, a social contract (more often unclear and unspoken) drives all our relationship behaviors: how we collaborate, how we treat each other, what is said and unsaid, our ways of engagement, and even what processes and tools we use to interact. It determines what questions we address and those we do not. The right social contract is the backbone of the success of the team. Some call this a culture, but I find those discussions too vague and distant from the daily workings of a team. I like to think of it as a contract among teammates that can be surgically engineered at the team level to hold each other accountable for the application of the agreed-upon practices that help the new contract be adhered to and sustained. The success of the whole team is not just achieved by one or two individuals changing behavior, not even the leader. It must involve everyone on the team agreeing that there are old notions of our behavior that no longer serve us in the world we live in today and must be left behind through the adoption of new proven practices. Engineering the move to teamship begins with an open discussion and renegotiation of the existing social contract for each of the 10 shifts among the team. As we explore each shift in the chapters to come, we will explore how to open the discussion about the new social contract for the shift and the high-return practices that support it.

This very first shift, the awakening to Co-elevation behaviors, is less in the doing. It's a new awareness, an awakening to the hope and possibility that a new set of behaviors and level of performance is possible—the awareness of the responsibility of being a high-performing teammate. To achieve that awakening we use a high-return teamship practice called recontracting that we will keep revisiting in each chapter for each shift. Simply, it's the process of discussing the current and possible new social contract for Co-elevation and agreeing to give the high-return teamship practices being introduced a try.

When this process starts, there is often a lot to overcome. Some teams have pockets of resentment that make them resistant to each other's input and ideas. They believe talking behind each other's backs is acceptable. As I mentioned before, some just coexist, each maximizing for their individual responsibilities and trying not to impose unless they need to collaborate in places where their work overlaps. In reality, the diversity of others' input is not really valued. This, and worse, up and down the 10 shifts, is a likely place we find the average team. Unfortunately, so much is lost through these old hidden team contracts, these assumptions of acceptable working relationships. The Co-elevating social contract is about leaning into an entirely higher commitment of performance and service among the team. But given a lifetime of old assumptions lived out every day, do we even know what serving each other as Co-elevating teammates would look like? What would it be like to put all these behavioral shifts together? And how do we call attention and awaken to where we could and should shift to a new set of team beliefs and practices? We use a diagnostic tool with twenty questions and a 0–5 scoring system to begin recontracting: this lets us open the discussion with teams about their purposefully engineered social contract and then, unlike detached conversations about culture and values, we can audit our progress every month through observing and discussing the adoption of simple high-return teamship practices. These diagnostic questions span the 10 shifts to teamship. You will find the diagnostic questions associated with a shift, and how to discuss them with your team, in the relevant chapter. The full list of diagnostic questions is also in the appendix.

An interesting side note: one of the problems we have found is that we are so ingrained to accept the behavior of teams today, if we send the diagnostic tool out before talking about what each question means and what the new standard really represents in practice, the results are quite different. A question like "Do we challenge each other when it's risky to do so?" receives a fairly high score if asked without a discussion among the team first, as people have really never thought about how this degree of candid discussion would work or show up relative to the current work of the team. But if we can explain what that question looks like when a team really does stretch its level of candor and risk-taking with each other, and give it context before answering the question, the score is quite a bit lower.

Giving the question texture for the team to consider is important. Texture like: "When there's something that you disagree with, but it's an emotionally charged item, do we just 'Let it slide'?" Or perhaps giving an example we all see every day, like "If we leave a room, do the real conversations start to happen in the walk down the hallway?" can elicit more accurate responses. Do our inside voices get a real hearing in real time? When we know there is a lack of alignment, do we just assume it will be ironed out later? Do we sometimes see people exercise their pocket veto by staying silent and doing something different than what was discussed? Do we have those "meetings after the meeting"? Are there private DMs during a meeting about the topic?

We have come to be so lulled into accepting mediocre teams, we don't notice that we lack professional integrity in our social contract; we are too far from being able to imagine what good could look like to be dissatisfied with how we are behaving. Similarly, when we coach a team over months to a level of Co-elevation, we find that sometimes the second time they take the diagnostic the answers are lower in some areas because the team has come to realize what real feedback to each other looks like, or how to hold each other accountable. Then the third diagnostic is much higher, as that awakening coupled with the application of the high-return practices is exactly what the team needed to elevate.

Having a transparent unveiling of the teammates' existing social contract with the results of the diagnostic and engaging in healthy discussion among the team about the state of the team's behaviors is always a great place to start. This diagnostic walk-through and discussion are the beginning of a commitment of the team to a new Co-elevation social contract.

RED FLAG RULES AND RED FLAG REPLAYS

Red Flag Rules are a team's simply worded and easy-to-remember rules of engagement for each of the 10 shifts that are agreed to as part of the new social contract. Red Flag Rules are about how we should be with one another. The Red Flag Rules are commitments we make to our teammates to work together and interpersonally engage in ways that help to land each of the 10 teamship shifts. A Red Flag Replay, then, is something we do regularly, ideally once a month, which looks back and asks, how are we doing with our commitments to our Red Flag Rules and the practices we agreed on to get there? Have we slipped into the old social contract behaviors and violated these new agreements? Do we need to humbly call out where we could have used the high-return teamship practices better? Everyone is asked to prepare for this discussion, and we should celebrate those who call themselves out to the team as an act of commitment and understanding that we are all human and we will make mistakes and keep growing together. There is no expectation of perfection and no shame in growing from our mistakes. The Red Flag Rule for the shift from hub-and-spoke to the leader to Co-elevation is: "We are equally committed to all goals of the team and each other to get there."

From now on, every chapter has a Red Flag Rule and a section about recontracting to help the team explore what the shift means to them before taking the diagnostic. You will also find the full list of rules in the appendix.

As we mentioned in chapter 1, with any change program it's tempting to fall back into old habits. Nominating a teamship ambassador within the team from the start to work alongside the leader and the team to advocate for the new behaviors and practices will help encourage adoption. It's every team-mate's job to go on this journey. It's every teammate's job to commit to higher performance and higher standards of team behavior. It's not one person's job. But someone empowered on the team to encourage and play coach at the beginning will help to speed up the shifts.

FROM HIRING STARS TO FORMING A CONSTELLATION

A new teamship social contract was required if Sergey Young's team was going to achieve their 10x growth target—and fulfill his ambition of having more time for his longevity fund. For instance, under the existing team contract, the idea that they would challenge each other in front of Young was highly unlikely. The idea that they would ever openly challenge Young's opinion? That was impossible. We worked through our diagnostic exercise that benchmarked Young's senior team against the world-class standard. I gave color to each diagnostic question and brought to life each of the shifts of teamship. I encouraged them to answer the diagnostic questions without fear or embarrassment. It's an anonymous process. Young reinforced, "How we say we behave is just a benchmark on a journey we can take together, and it's our decision as a team how far and how fast we want to go." The scores were low. I then asked three questions:

➤ Is where we are acceptable to us?

➤ When taking the diagnostic, where particularly did you feel you needed to shift and relinquish some old ways of working that may not serve you well?

➤ Are you willing to contract/pledge to one another to adopt new ways drawn from these points?

As one of Young's executives told me months later, "The opportunity became clear that the adoption of new ways of working was the only way we could meet Young's seemingly outrageous growth goals. If everyone brought our biggest issues to the table and collectively worked together to an aligned goal, instead of just individually killing ourselves to satisfy Young, the outrageous goals soon didn't seem as outrageous." As for Young, he says, "I was quickly able to dedicate more time to strategy and investor relations for the core VC business while also developing my new passion project. My job shifted toward making sure the team grew and felt supported by each other rather than feeling like they were hunkered down and being accountable only to me. The coaching freed up about a third of my time and allowed us to both meet the original goals and for me to start an entirely new business." The truth is, teamship freed up that time and put Young's extraordinary goals within reach.

CHAPTER 3

SHIFTING FROM CONFLICT AVOIDANCE TO CANDOR

Red Flag Rule:
We speak courageously.

Welcome to the Things That Matter Outlier Team Meeting. This isn't the time or place for parade laps about how well the team is doing. There are times for that too, but not now, not here," says Bill Connors, president of Xfinity for Comcast Cable, the largest broadband and pay TV operator in the United States. "Everybody's airing their dirty laundry. Everyone is talking about everyone's problems and everybody's focus is on how to get these operational problems fixed." If an outsider joined the meeting partway through and heard the ongoing discussion, from the candor and collaboration, they would find it hard to know who really owned any one problem. If they had a week of critical operations outages, the head of marketing will just as likely offer advice and make recommendations that contribute to the solution from their perspective in the spirit of helping their teammate. If there has been a falloff in demand, the head of finance can be among the strongest voices offering insight and support. If there are multimillion-dollar gaps in the accounts to fill, the head of digital experiences is expected to have ideas because it's a collective effort to find the right solution. They're certainly not staying in their swim lanes and allowing a teammate to fail. If we're part of the leadership team, everyone is in everyone else's role to be immersive in the total business outcomes because it's the team's responsibility to call out any and all failures in performance and have accretive ideas for business success and innovation, wherever they may be needed. In world-class teams, up to 30 percent of our attention is committed to the needs of the wider enterprise, not just our own division.

We will describe in detail the practice of Things That Matter Outlier Team Meetings later in the chapter, but they have been a feature of Connors's working week at Comcast for more than four decades. They're a signature of his approach to teamship that has seen his career trajectory rise from the company's broadband operation in Singapore, to leading as the senior executive of all US Eastern, Midwest, and Central Divisions, to running the enterprise of more than 52 million customers and $60 billion in revenue. During his eleven years as president of the Central Division, he took these historically challenged geographies, as they relate to market share and financial performance, from under- to outperforming every other business unit and becoming the market share growth engine of the business and largest individual EBITDA contributor among all business units in the Comcast/NBCUniversal family of assets. The Things That Matter Outlier Team Meeting is Connors's way of creating a culture of candor—candor about issues that drive results. People often say to *praise in public but challenge in private*. Well, that misses the opportunity to have the challenge triangulated with other people's insights. If I feel some initiative has undue risk but I decide to take my feedback "offline" to deliver it to you later in private, I'm missing the chance to give my feedback publicly and have it debated by other members of the team, for my insights to either gain traction or be rebutted by the greater wisdom of the team. That old belief of praising in public but challenging in private is for a team of sensitive, perhaps defensive, individuals who have not agreed to leverage the team to sharpen and stress-test each other's ideas. "The Things That Matter Outlier Meeting isn't easy when it's first introduced to a team," says Connors. "For so many, it is almost impossible to stay on the agenda because they always want to say something like, 'We just won four awards for our last project.' Truly fantastic, but not for now. Then, when you start to see the outlier items start coming off the list; when you start to get better results—real operating results—confidence builds and there's more understanding of the reason for the hard-core approach. *Oh! Now I get why we're doing this.*" Connors describes the meeting as essential to senior team candor and setting the tone for a broader, organizational operating culture that is willing to talk courageously about what needs to be fixed and who needs to fix it. "We certainly applaud goals that are going well and the amazing work ethic and say thank you," says Connors. "And yet we keep coming back and talking about all the things that are not on pace and the things that are underdelivering. If you do that, you can start to condition the whole employee base with being comfortable with candor and setting a new standard for high-performing teams."

BANNING THE BACK CHANNEL

World-class teams know that sunlight is the best disinfectant. We need to awaken to candor and realize how erosive conflict avoidance is to a team. We miss bold innovations and expose the organization to unnecessary risks when opportunities and threats are not transparently articulated. The old team social contract is to not speak up for fear of throwing a peer under the bus, but the new social contract is not holding back for fear of letting your peer struggle and fail without the value of your opinion. But too many teams are stuck in those old behaviors. Despite my friend Kim Malone Scott's hard work on *Radical Candor* to rid teams of such behaviors, it is still rife and we are in need of new candor practices.

Our research shows that 72 percent of team members

avoid conflict. Too many teams speak critically in discrete private conversations. The "meeting that takes place after the meeting" is a real source of candor and transparency—but it should happen in the meeting itself. The problem can go as far as the rampant talking behind each other's backs that we were warned about as bad form when we were in the schoolyard, yet is still present in some of the most prestigious corridors of power. Senior leaders who permit back-channel conversation are allowing what our research shows is the most draining behavior of high-performing teams and causes the greatest erosion to shareholder value. Teamship is a shift to a social contract to care enough about each other's success that we withhold nothing from the team that might stand in the way of the best solutions. In our diagnostic, the average team is a 2.4 on a 5-point scale in candor. Using high-return practices to create psychological safety that allows them to stress-test each other's ideas openly in service of the mission, teams can reach 4.5 on that 5-point scale for candor in just six months.

CANDOR IGNITES DECISION-MAKING

One team where world-class candor is prized is the leadership team at iHeartMedia, run by chairman and CEO Bob Pittman. Pittman has earned Hall of Fame status in the media industry. He was the cofounder and programmer behind the launch of MTV in 1981 and was a pioneer of cable networks as former CEO of MTV Networks; he was CEO of AOL Networks when 50 percent of all internet traffic was through AOL as it brought the internet to the mass market and then he went on to become chief operating officer of AOL Time Warner. iHeart is the number one audio company in the United States, reaching nine out of ten Americans every month, either on its network of 860+ live broadcast radio stations, its digital platforms, including the iHeartRadio app, or its booming podcast business. Like Connors, Pittman has always believed that candor in service of effective team decision-making is vital. But Pittman has gone a step further. He has made dissent one of iHeart's corporate values. "We welcome dissent across the team and want to hear it because it's essential," says Pittman. "Interdisciplinary dissent is always about the solutions to a real challenge, it's not saying *'That's useless, I don't like it, I don't believe it, that will never work.'* That's just grumbling. Proper dissent can be pointing out that something might not work because *'I have this insight you may not have from your vantage point or experiences, and I also have this idea to consider.'*" Meetings are the space for wrestling with problems that need to be solved. Any problem. "Also, don't say anything in my office you wouldn't say in the STRATCOM meeting, which is our senior meeting," says Pittman. "And I don't want a recitation of what you've done. Please don't bring that to that meeting. Bring exceptions, bring places where you are struggling, and bring places where others are holding you up. We need to focus on what's going better and why, what's going worse and what we can do. And let's really dig into those issues as a team where we have a richer set of opinions from different experiences that might build a breakthrough solution." And not to put too fine a point on it, but nothing is to be heard behind closed doors that can't be addressed with the team, especially conflict between executives. "If you've got something that you can't work out with someone else, escalate that in the meeting," says Pittman. "No matter where you're stuck, we can unstick it." He says that, contrary to what most people think, being open and direct is the ultimate show of respect. It may not be comfortable or easy at first. "But it shows that we are all committed to the shared mission and each other. That means we won't let each other fail—and it also means we have to share our data points of concern and challenge," says Pittman.

TEAMSHIP PRACTICES

After completing the diagnostic and establishing the Red Flag Rule, six teamship practices support the shift from conflict avoidance to candor, including two teamship practices that are fundamental behaviors of every world-class team, the Power of Three and Stress Testing.

1. **The Power of Three:** Unlocking candor by breaking down meetings into smaller groups (typically three-strong) to tackle specific issues before reporting back.
2. **Stress Testing:** A superfood of world-class teams that

battle-hardens ideas/proposals but also identifies ways team members can help them fly.

3. **Candor Break:** A quick way to check what's not being said that needs to be said in a meeting.

4. **Outlier Meetings:** Bill Connors's proven weekly team meeting to identify what needs to be fixed.

5. **Yoda in the Room:** When there's a tough or volatile situation, here's a safe word and process to speak hard truths.

6. **Hiring Candor:** Creating a culture of candor starts from the moment you hire talent and it's about how you show up in the interview as much as the candidate.

The Candor Diagnostic

STEP ONE: *Team Discussion About Candor*

Working with Pittman's team at iHeart, I asked, "Let's look around the room. Does everyone have the ability to challenge each other? If somebody has a challenge to what Trevor is doing, can we share that? Can we comfortably wrestle and debate in the open? I'm not just talking about when Bob calls a meeting specifically about a topic. Are we proactive in voicing our full critical voice here as needed when it might feel socially risky to do so?" The iHeart team all saw they had room to develop here. In fact, when they went into breakout rooms after the diagnostic to discuss what needed to change, one of the executives openly acknowledged they had recently participated in back-channel conversation that didn't serve the team and agreed to commit to changing behavior over the next month. The team agreed and the one-month challenge among the team was on!

STEP TWO: *Diagnostic Questions*
All team members give a 1 to 5 score for the following questions (1: Strongly disagree, 2: Disagree, 3: Neutral, 4: Agree, 5: Strongly agree):

➤ All team members are willing to directly challenge one another, even when it is risky to do so, or the topic is outside their "swim lane" or area of expertise.

➤ All team members actively hold each other accountable for one another's commitments and outcomes.

The diagnostic must be administered by a team member who is seen as agnostic and trusted, as the scoring is private and will not be attributed to individuals. Use an online survey tool or the Diagnostic Assessment on my website. Our research shows that world-class teams score 4.5 out of 5 for the candor diagnostic.

Red Flag Rule and Red Flag Replays

A month later at our next transformation meeting with Pittman's team, we used the Red Flag Replay teamship practice to check our progress toward our Red Flag Rule of "we speak courageously" and whether the new social contract had been violated since our previous session. The goal was to put violations out there and discuss them. Again, another member of the team admitted to talking behind the back of a teammate and committed to talking to their peer about it. Openly discussing our violation of any of those new social contracts is a big step for many teams to build momentum for the shift and trust among the team.

Reflecting in later Red Flag Replays, Pittman celebrated: "Sometimes, people who are at an impasse are now coming to the STRATCOM meeting not to get adjudication but to get a broader airing for better clarity. The reality is that conversations in the shadows or among just two parties usually have incomplete information. Bringing the issue to STRATCOM assures we have the entirety of the team weighing in creating value from the interdependencies of the team." Looking back, Pittman's team understood and embraced the need for a new social contract for candor at iHeart. What brought their new teamship behaviors to life was the diligent adoption of high-return practices.

The simple Red Flag Rule for team behavior that might be agreed for candor is: "We speak courageously." Calling a monthly Red Flag Replay as the team works through the following teamship practices will help to check whether or not everyone is abiding by the new social contract and adopting the new behaviors of teamship.

Teamship Practice: The Power of Three

One of the most powerful yet overlooked practices of team collaboration is the Power of Three. By breaking the whole team into smaller groups of three people—even just for five to eight minutes—you unleash massive psychological safety. In these small groups, whether they are when teams are together in an office or working virtually, people have more courage to share openly. In a large meeting room, it can be as simple as turning chairs toward each other for smaller group discussions. Chapter 6 will explore collaboration and the elevation of psychological safety in more depth, but our data shows that candor in small breakout rooms is 85 percent higher than when teams meet as a single cohort in a main room. In smaller groups, individuals will self-critique and weed out weak ideas. Then when they come back into the bigger room and are asked about the discussion they have just had, they are unlikely to water their group's consensus down too much, for fear of losing face and admitting to their peers that they have broken the social contract of candor and transparency. Asking the breakout groups to write down their insights in a shared document helps to capture that candor for everyone to see. Pittman says the belief that people want to speak openly in meetings with larger teams is a real miss. "I used to think that we would have good healthy discussions in rooms of fifteen people," he says. "Then you'd go out of the meeting and see two people in a hallway saying what really needed to be said in the room we just walked out of, but they didn't have the time or confidence. When we use small conversation pods, we get a more fulsome view of what's happening and a much better debate. If we don't use it, I know where the truth will be found, it'll be out in the hallway after the meeting, and we will all suffer from it."

Teamship Practice: Stress Testing

The teamship practice of regular Stress Testing is truly the superfood of a high-performing team. Our new social contract is to adopt a challenge culture, a clear *see something, say something* agreement. One of the greatest drains to the old culture was the all-too-common "report out," which forced teams to sit through hours of those twenty-page decks that someone reads through while only a couple of people chime in. Most sit in silence or respond to emails during those presentations, and if some do have a dissenting point of view they often decide to hold off and lobby for their point afterward, or perhaps never voice their thoughts due to concerns that it is outside their swim lane or it just won't be appreciated. *Dream teams don't do that.* Stress Testing is a core process that can radically introduce and elevate entirely different modes of collaboration and agile working, as we will see in chapter 7.

The Stress Testing practice turns building a world-class challenge culture into a clear and precise assignment, not left to chance, or waiting for the entire mindset and culture of a team to change. Here's how it works: A team member presents a high-priority project in a team meeting. Unlike a typical "report out" they are limited to a very short presentation, ideally only one slide, outlining:

➤ What's perceived to have been achieved so far?
➤ Where are they *struggling* (the use of the word here is important, as it mandates sharing vulnerability and

an invitation to the group of support through their advice)?

➤ What's planned for the next phase of work?

The team is told to listen to this from the perspective of a mandate to stress-test where the individual is and where they are going. It's very important to note and discuss before the exercise that this is not an invitation to hijack the person's accountability or authority. Instead, it's the commitment to give them the benefit of double-barrel feedback to heighten the chances of success; to assure they see the risks and opportunities you see, and that they do not fail; and to give them the richest set of inputs to consider.

Next, team members are sent into breakout rooms (if in a virtual meeting) or turn chairs toward each other in groups of three. The small groups are asked to document their insights and advice and offer no-holds-barred feedback and constructive criticism in the following simple format:

1. What challenges or risks do those in the breakout group see from what was presented?
2. What suggested innovations or advice might they offer?
3. What offers of support or help do they want to give?

The three-person groups work collectively to give all their input to ensure the success of their colleague, with no rock left unturned in the time allotted, which can be set to correlate with the complexity of the issue at hand, with simple issues taking less time. Groups challenge anything that might involve unacceptable or unnecessarily high levels of risk, brainstorm ways to mitigate that risk, and of course maintain a respectful, collegial tone. It's essential to capture feedback from the breakout rooms/small groups in a shared document divided into columns for challenges, innovations, and offers of help. This ensures that the person responsible for the project has clear, well-documented input encompassing a variety of perspectives along with concrete offers of support. Writing at a sufficient degree of specificity is an art that the team will develop, and some, as you will see later, choose to move this feedback opportunity to before or after the meeting, therefore giving everyone abundant time to consider all input. This practice ensures that by the time the project comes to fruition, it has been subject to rigorous examination and benefits from the entire wisdom of the team.

Once teams share their feedback, it is essential for the recipient to, in real time or perhaps as a follow-up at a later time, give those who have contributed a clear reaction and response to their input, offering a summary of what was shared with a *Yes, I will do this,* a *No, and here's why not,* or a *Maybe, and we need to do further research before making a decision.* This Yes/No/Maybe is an important bow to tie at the end of this exercise and again assures that full transparency exists and the perception that this process hijacks authority is not present.

Teamship Practice: Candor Break

Let's imagine an executive team is discussing a change to their remote work policy to possibly insist that associates spend more of their time in the office. They seem to have all agreed that bringing people back is a great idea.

Tom, the CFO, says: "We need to be sure everyone is being productive with their time and deadlines are being met, that there's no slacking off. It's easier to do that when everyone is in the office."

Tania, the COO, says: "Exactly, Tom, and what's the point of having all this real estate if no one is here using it?"

No one speaks against the idea. There's no apparent dissent.

Candor breaks are the fastest and best way to discover, in real time, what is being held back. It's the antidote to lazy, perhaps passive consensus. To do so, regularly pause the meeting to ask the team, *What's not being said in this room that should be said?* Ask for a candor break. Instruct team members to turn to their neighbor and answer this question—or go to a virtual breakout room. Open a shared cloud document in each discussion pod to catalog thoughts and ideas in real time. Then share what was captured with the whole group when you return to the main room. If you want to know what wasn't being said about a return-to-office policy—what a candor break might have brought to the surface—read on and you will find the answers in chapter 6.

Teamship Practice: Outlier Meetings

Bill Connors's Things That Matter Outlier Team Meetings are scheduled for one hour a week and always have the same agenda to keep the team focused on what matters to the business. In Connors's case, the agenda is organized around

Xfinity's organizational priorities, which are represented by the acronym CENTER, as in Center Culture:

➤ Customer Growth
➤ EBITDA
➤ Net Promoter Scores
➤ Top-line Revenue
➤ Employee Engagement
➤ Return on Capital

One at a time, the team is asked to flag outlier issues under each of these areas in turn and be prepared for candid discussion. If there's an operational issue that isn't going to be resolved this week, it stays on the agenda and is discussed until it *is* resolved. "The one-hour speed requirement helps to elevate the dialogue as well as cut out wasted motion," says Connors.

Teamship Practice: Yoda in the Room

Another practice is inspired by Yoda, the wise Jedi master from the Star Wars films, who represents ultimate wisdom, truth, and insight—all the answers we need in one entity. I believe the wisdom of Yoda is in every team but not in any one of us alone. Only by drawing out of everyone their point of view can we achieve the best, boldest answers. The problem is that most people don't have the courage to speak up. So, you're going to make Yoda the "safe word" for business. In time we want every team member to be an active Yoda. But to begin, you can appoint a few Yodas in any meeting or group conversation, though it is particularly useful in potentially difficult or volatile situations. By giving the Yodas explicit permission to raise their hand and call a "Yoda moment," and say the hard things or act as a referee between competing perspectives, you are making it safe for others to do the same. Taking time to introduce the Yoda concept and to select some Yodas for the role goes a long way to diffusing tension in challenging conversations before it hinders candor and ultimately your business results.

To pilot this practice, ask for a volunteer or volunteers to be the Yoda(s) for the session. When choosing Yodas, remember, they do not need to be the most senior people in the room. Rather, they should be people who are known for having good judgment and being fair.

If you're not sure if your team or the people in your meeting will be open to appointing a Yoda, that may indicate a lack of candor or safety in the group, which means you really could benefit from having one.

At your next meeting, set aside approximately five minutes to introduce the Yoda concept. Discuss how having a Yoda might benefit your team dynamic and results.

Here's how a Yoda moment might play out:

It's that moment when Suki, Sally, or Julio raises their hand and says, "Yoda moment," and the leader says, "Okay, go for it."

Suki says, "Well, it seems we have circled this topic so many times and never landed the plane. Are we really getting anywhere or perhaps are we avoiding addressing the real problem at hand, which is . . ."

Or Sally simply points out what often happens in meetings: "It seems the conversation has gone way off topic and into a rabbit hole that is tangential and may be better dealt with offline? Perhaps we should get back to the agenda?"

Or Julio says: "I may be off base, but we are talking about Pierre's division, and we have not heard at all from him in a while. Pierre, what are you thinking?"

You get the idea. The Yoda word gives every member of the meeting the responsibility for the meeting's success and for greater transparency of the discussion. Too often we sit in failing dialogues and do not think it's our role or responsibility to call it out. In a Co-elevating team, it's everyone's job to assure the success of the meeting, and if there is something you can say to get to a better outcome faster, then it's your responsibility to say it.

A Yoda moment is an invitation to say what needs to be said. It's an open invitation to say the bold thing you are thinking but typically would keep to yourself, or would direct message in a chat, or share as you're walking down the hall after the meeting has finished.

Teamship Practice: Hiring Candor

Investor, entrepreneur, and *Principles* author Ray Dalio is renowned for his belief in radical honesty and radical transparency at the asset management business Bridgewater Associates, which he ran for almost fifty years, until 2022, growing the company from the two-bedroom apartment where he lived in 1975 to a $120 billion firm. Talking to Dalio at Davos about putting his principles into practice, he shared that he believes it is easiest to do when you hire people experienced and innately comfortable with such candor, as most companies struggle mightily to make this shift with the average existing population. Dalio says you should "show your warts" during interviews and give candidates a firsthand taste of your culture of candor. He advocates being candid with candidates about the challenges the organization faces. He doesn't advocate selling the vacancy, but being honest about how tough the job is going to be. "Show your job prospects the real picture, especially the bad stuff. Also show them the principles in action, including the most difficult aspects. That way you will stress-test their willingness to endure the real challenges," says Dalio. When leaders are down to the final candidate, they should also be candid about any reservations they have about that person's qualifications and gauge the candidate's reaction to the feedback. If you see gaps or challenges in a potential hire, point them out as well as ask them to express their concerns about the role and the company. This allows you to see before making the hire if they will approach candor and transparency in real time.

FEEDBACK IS A GIFT

The biggest challenge with introducing a peer-to-peer challenge culture is that, with the exception of some sports teams in the locker room at halftime, we have never really had experience with giving or getting feedback fluidly from peers. Since we were children, feedback came from authority figures, and we were expected to do something with it. To do what we were told, by our parents, by our teachers, by our coaches, by our bosses. But the feedback from our peers is different. It does not come with a contract of assumed responsibility to execute it all. It's all just data, and it is our responsibility to collect it courageously, analyze it, and then do with it what we feel is appropriate. Of course, if over time someone in authority sees our inability to take such feedback, then they may step in, but feedback is a gift, and the recipient has the right to do with it what they wish. The key to our success is its transparent and full collection and analysis. The social contract of candor from peers is something we have to get used to giving and receiving, and regular Stress Testing is the active coaching we give each other to adopt the new challenge culture.

CANDOR AS A STEP TOWARD DEEPER RELATIONSHIPS

Understanding that candor and candid feedback is a gift is part of the team's journey toward Co-elevation. They are part of a world-class team's commitment to be of service to each other and to care about each other to want to go higher together. It's a step toward deeper, more purposeful relationships, as we will see in the next chapter.

CHAPTER 4

SHIFTING FROM SERENDIPITOUS RELATIONSHIPS TO PURPOSEFUL TEAM BOND-BUILDING

Red Flag Rule:
We are truly committed to one another.

P edro Carrilho and his business partner Juan Martin were facing a classic entrepreneurs' problem. They were smart, focused, and had a clear vision for their tech start-up PhoenixDX, a low-code solutions business based in Sydney, Australia. Under their close leadership, the business grew rapidly. But hands-on engagement from founders can only take a start-up so far; there was no way they could scale if the highly effective collaboration they had created at the top did not cascade down into the company. As cofounders, they cared deeply about each other and could practically complete each other's sentences. However, when they looked at the level below them, they didn't see the same tight-knit bonding that had happened organically between them. Instead, they saw a business growing in functional silos and misunderstanding, with people working hard on their part of the process but without worrying too much about what everyone else was doing and with very little trust between the teams. They knew they needed help. "We also didn't want a business full of Pedritos and little Juans. We needed people who would challenge us and each other like we did as founders." Carrilho and Martin believed wholeheartedly in Co-elevation; they just needed a way to start bringing it to life in their teams.

Like any business that involves consultancy around a design-and-build solution, you need sales, project management, and engineering (in this case the developers, who were working remotely across different Asia Pacific countries) to work as one customer-centric team. "But we looked at each other as mere tiles on a screen," one of the team members recalled. "I may work with this person occasionally. I barely work with this one. *We were barely a team that knew each other, let alone cared.*" Because of this breakdown, Martin and Carrilho were working hard, spinning wheels to close customer-experience gaps, intervening in existing projects rather than spending their time on strategy and initiatives to grow the business. We needed to build deeper relationships where there were only fragments before. The team below the founders needed to care enough about each other not to let each other fail. They needed to invest in creating empathy and personal trust. The challenge was to transform PhoenixDX in six months.

RELATIONSHIPS AND TRUST ARE THE FOUNDATIONS OF TRANSFORMATION

Only 41 percent of team members believe caring, trusting, and supportive relationships exist with their peers. Fifty-eight percent of employees say that they trust strangers more than they trust their own associates at work. Building relationships among team members on a foundation of commitment and empathy is critical to providing an environment of forgiveness and caring enough to challenge each other. Often teams have pockets of broken trust between peers, and left unchecked, this can develop into deep resentments that erode shareholder value. Yet all too often, the team sits by seemingly helplessly enduring poor results, behavior, and performance. Do you know of a breakdown in personal relationships in your team that is holding back company performance?

Traditionally, bond-building happened when someone walked down the hall and bumped into another person at the watercooler. It was organic. That's why we hear leaders say they want to see people get back to the office; they want that kind of culture-building to happen. But the problem with this traditional form of relationship-building, which we might call serendipitous bond-building, is that it happens by chance. It's exactly the kind of accidental bond-building we need to move away from. It was fine in an analog age, but it's nowhere near effective enough for today. We don't have time to rely on serendipity when global teams who are expected to perform audacious tasks quickly are thrown together and reshaped constantly, often with no history together and with online platforms as the primary form of engagement. Serendipitous bond-building won't cut it anymore. Instead, we need leaders like Drew Houston, the CEO at Dropbox, who put their mind to engineering culture, purposefully building their cultures and not letting teams' connectedness be taken for granted. As we will see in the next chapter, Houston shifted Dropbox to a virtual-first business, moving from ten physical spaces to thirty global neighborhoods, where instead of an office, he had small studios of collaboration space geared for meaningful in-person connection. When Dropboxers get together in the same place, it's to deepen relationships. But our research shows that leaders like Drew who lean in to engineer the behaviors of their teams are the exception. Indicative of this, only 49 percent of team members respect and value what their peers contribute. Without a basic underlying commitment of professional respect, it is no wonder we see significant gaps in almost every team in high-integrity professional behaviors like candor. Relationships are the foundation of all productive interaction. Why? Because of trust.

PERSONAL, PROFESSIONAL, AND STRUCTURAL TRUST

Trust exists in three different types: professional trust, structural trust, and personal trust. The way this comes to life the most for me is in an interaction that I witnessed when I was a young man. My first job right out of college was working at a manufacturing plant in Wilmington, Delaware. One day, the union leader came into the office to talk to the new plant manager. He said, "Hey, Joe, I've done my research and I have to say, you're a pretty good egg. I called around a bunch of other plants you've managed, and I'm glad to have you here. But here's what we need to do. We need to go have a drink." I recognized how the union leader started off by acknowledging that he has respect for and trust in the new plant manager on a professional basis, based on his reputation of doing good work. But beyond that professional trust, the union leader was acknowledging that they needed to develop a personal relationship and be able to talk on the side when their representatives didn't want them to. He meant that they needed to develop personal trust, the kind where you can look somebody in the eye and really believe them, know their values, know that they're being honest, and know they have high integrity and that they care. Then as the union leader left the room, he turned back and said, "All that's great, by the way, but I'm still likely to make your life hell," and chuckled. That last statement was about structural trust—accepting that their roles demand different perspectives since the union leader's job may at times be at odds with the plant manager's. There are lots of structural breakdowns in organizations: boss and subordinate, functions that may have more power than others, or, like the case with the union leader and plant manager, teams whose priorities may sometimes clash. But at the end of the day, that union leader was so right. It's the personal relationship that allows you to cut through disagreements and structural impediments and build the kind of trust you need to work collaboratively. For example, a head of engineering and a head of marketing are going to see the world differently professionally. As a result, they then have to work together personally to find common ground and to move things forward when difficulties arise. Some people think that this is only something that's done organically or accidentally. That's not the case. For years at Ferrazzi Greenlight we have been opening teams that have been broken, that have held old resentments within them, and, through targeted work, we have moved them to being committed to each other.

Trust is foundational to change. As leaders and as teams we need to embrace and recognize this. Repeated use of Stress Testing, the teamship practice we described in the last chapter, is a great way to build professional trust, because the more a team exercises candor and spends the time to see what each other is thinking, the more they grow in their respect for each other and stop dismissing each other because of seemingly different beliefs. Thoughts like *Well, sure they did, because they were trained differently, and they experienced different things* too often lead to a breakdown of trust and to disrespect when they *should* lead to curiosity. If in a meeting a friend says something you don't agree with, you might say, "Hey, what are you talking about?" Respect is assumed because you are friends. But if in a meeting someone you don't know says something you disagree with, you may just stay quiet, thinking to yourself that they have their head up their back end. It's the personal relationship and the new social contract that allow us to dig deeper to get to the truth. We need to build that relationship and we need to negotiate the social contract.

In my previous books, *Never Eat Alone* and *Leading Without Authority*, I talked about trust, the importance of generosity, and the idea of Serve, Share, and Care. Now I want to talk about that in the context of teamship. So, let's start with service. In chapter 2 we talked about a commitment to service (Co-elevation) as the benchmark for a high-performing team—the commitment to elevate others, to serve each other as a team. My friend the organizational psychologist Adam Grant read *Never Eat Alone* when he was a grad student. In it I talk about how critical it is in a network to lead with generosity, and Adam has done extraordinary research proving that to go higher in this world, the fastest way to accelerate your own success is to be generous to others. How can you understand another person's career objectives and help them achieve them; how can you just listen and be there as their coach? (We will talk more about that in chapter 10.) It's the same among teams. Team members need to know their social obligations and then how they *can serve each other*.

We also need to start focusing on sharing with each other. Sharing taps into one another's humanity. I may not be exactly like you, but if I walk in your shoes through sharing and shared storytelling, I can empathize with you and begin to understand your perspective.

The last element is Care. Caring is a choice people can make. Once I know you care, I'll hear your ideas. Once I know you care and that you see me as an individual, I'll be fine with wrestling through tough collaborations and disagreements.

It's so important that we get our team to know that they've got to produce a higher degree of relational commitment among each other for all this to work—*and they are responsible for that*. If everybody says that they will grow to care about each other, that means that they will also grow to ask questions and be curious.

TEAMSHIP PRACTICES

After completing the diagnostic and establishing the Red Flag Rule, three teamship practices support the shift from serendipitous relationships to purposeful bond-building, including one of the most powerful practices we have coached teams all over the world to do, the Personal Professional Check-in.

1. **Sweet and Sour:** A five-minute check at the beginning of meetings to ask team members to share something that's going well and something that's more challenging in their life right now.

2. **Personal Professional Check-in:** This deeper check-in can forge instant bonds between strangers, but for teams it is often the tipping point for creating trust between peers.

3. **Intimacy Dinner:** A once-a-quarter dinner that's built around storytelling—the stories that made us who we are today.

The Relationship Diagnostic

STEP ONE: *Team Discussion on Our Relationships*

As I did for the iHeart team in the previous chapter, someone believed to be trusted and relatively impartial on the team must facilitate this diagnostic exercise, which, each time, opens up the discussion about their relationships. Ideally, the team will have read this chapter and come prepared to discuss the examples relative to our current behaviors and social contract relative to our relationships. Do we have the kind of relationships of service, sharing, and caring we find in world-class Co-elevating teams? Our twenty years of diagnostic data show that the average relationship score for teams is 2.8 on a 5-point scale. That figure dipped to 2.3 during the pandemic unless teams invested in purposeful bonding. World-class teams score 4.7. But why are the scores so low for teams when it comes to respecting and valuing each other or establishing committed relationships of service? Most team relationships are built on serendipity rather than purpose. That was what we found when we ran our diagnostic exercise at PhoenixDX. The cross-functional teams scored 2.4 on the 5-point scale for relationships. They needed to adopt teamship practices.

STEP TWO: *Diagnostic Questions*
All team members give a score of 1 to 5 for the following questions (1: Strongly disagree, 2: Disagree, 3: Neutral, 4: Agree, 5: Strongly agree):

➤ All team members respect and value what every other member of this team contributes.
➤ All team members have established caring, trusting, and supportive relationships with all other members of this team.
➤ All team members proactively deepen and improve their relationships with the network of those critical to our success and turn associates important to the team into real advocates.

The diagnostic must be administered by a team member who is seen as agnostic and trusted, as the scoring is private and will not be attributed to individuals. Use an online survey tool or the Diagnostic Assessment on my website.

Red Flag Rule and Red Flag Replays
The Red Flag Rule for purposeful relationships is: "We are truly committed to one another." Calling for a Red Flag Replay on this particular shift within a month of practicing the below teamship practices and then regularly thereafter is an opportu-

nity to hold space to talk about where things may have gone off the rails, to check that our new behavioral commitments are being observed and teamship practices are being implemented.

Teamship Practice: Sweet and Sour

Empathy is what builds relationships. It's the gateway. And what's the key to opening up that gateway of empathy? Sharing vulnerably. So no longer is it Dwane from sales and Sasha from marketing. These are now people who have joy, celebration, struggles, challenges, fears, all of the things that make us human. We have to engineer this vulnerability in a practicable and very deliberate way. Take five minutes at the beginning of a meeting and do something I call Sweet and Sour. Everybody goes around and, very simply, shares what's going on most sweetly in their life right now and what has been most challenging recently. A Sweet could be that your son is doing really well in soccer, or your project has finally launched for the new HR system after all those months. A Sour could be that your mom is struggling right now, and you're worried about her since she is alone in Pittsburgh. Or you're so frustrated that budgeting delays are stalling your Q2 lead gen project and may jeopardize the results.

The thing about Sweet and Sour is that because you start with what is sweet, it tends to be easier for a team that is less comfortable with vulnerability. The Sour is not usually as sour after you share the Sweet; people tend to share something a bit less deep. And that's okay for this time and environment. We typically allow around a minute for each person to speak, so it can be fairly short.

Teamship Practice: Personal Professional Check-in

Personal Professional Check-in (PPC) is one of the most powerful things that we've coached teams all over the world to do. I even use it as the basis of professional dinners with executives that bring a group of strangers closer instantly. While Sweet and Sour is a minute per person, a PPC can be a couple of minutes a person or more depending on preference and setting (for example, over a team dinner versus in a weekly meeting).

To do a PPC is simple. Ask, "What's really going on for you? Where might you be struggling, personally and professionally?"

Because both of these questions are intended to reveal struggles, it can and often does elicit deeper responses. The key, of course, is who opens up the exercise. If it's the leader, be sure you have practiced, and you are laying an open path for the group to share their most authentic and vulnerable selves. Perhaps it's your aging parents. Or it could be a concern with health issues of someone close, or children who are struggling. I often shared about my foster children. The youngest came into my home at twelve. Before coming into our home, he had been in more than a dozen others. His life was tough and certain habits were deeply ingrained. And along the way, we've had some really tumultuous times—getting him to appreciate that we are there for him as family while he was scared and not wanting to embrace what has only hurt him in the past. There are so many things that we can share with each other in a PPC. What's important is that the person who goes first models the appropriate depth. If you don't feel that you have the ability to share openly and share vulnerably, then you might ask somebody on the team who does to go first.

We've seen this practice be the tipping point to transform team trust. There was a gentleman named Joseph, the head of fundraising of a prominent NGO we were coaching, who was a bit of a smart-ass wise guy whom many on the team didn't appreciate and some distrusted. He did his own thing in his own way but got results. During a PPC, he shared very vulnerably and openly about some health issues his wife was experiencing. His reflections were heartfelt and very raw. The team mirrored his sentiment, and it shifted people's perspectives; they were quicker to forgive his style as quirky. In fact, the head of marketing, who was particularly resentful of Joseph, ended up not only deepening their relationship from a professional standpoint but helping him get introduced to some medical professionals who were ultimately critical to Joseph's wife's recovery.

Teamship Practice: Intimacy Dinner

"What experience from your past has most contributed to who you are today?"

This question, shared openly among a team, invites vulnerable sharing of the defining moments of our lives, and again, if you are leading the exercise, please lead with something vulnerable. In some rooms I tell the story that I've told in my books, growing up as a poor kid with an unemployed steelworking dad and cleaning-lady mom and yet going to rich schools because my dad had talked the headmaster into a full scholarship. It's a story about my feeling of embarrassment and how, while it instilled a drive in me, it was tough on my relationship with my parents, as we were all ill-equipped to deal with difficult emotions and shame. With other teams, I might go a little deeper and talk about growing up as a Christian (I still am), realizing I was gay, and dealing with the shame of hiding it from my family and community for fear of rejection. How that experience made me feel and again how that drove me to constantly work harder and seek places where I felt I belonged.

The Intimacy Dinner is exactly what it sounds like. Once a quarter invite the team to a meal and over dinner get to know each other more deeply through this storytelling and sharing. It works as a round-robin. Have the first couple of people be volunteers to assure those who are ready go first and then just go around from there. You only need one question per dinner. Here are some questions that work well:

1. What experience from your past has most contributed to who you are today?
2. What can you do to free yourself to make room for going higher?
3. What's the biggest mistake you've made personally or professionally and the lesson you've learned from it?
4. Is there anything you are still holding on to that you need to let go of?
5. Is there anybody in your life you would like to make amends to?
6. What is the hardest lesson that you have learned?

7. What are you afraid you will not be able to accomplish in your lifetime?
8. What do you want team members to understand about you that they might not know?
9. What legacy would you like to leave personally and professionally?

Tips for a great dinner: Arrange for a perfectly quiet private room. Be sure everyone can see and hear each other at the table. Opt for whatever creates closer physical and emotional space. Don't let the chairs be too far from each other. Opt for chairs without arms and tables that do not have large centerpieces that prevent you from seeing each other easily. You want this to be very intimate. Talk to the waitstaff and ask them to come in rarely, and when they do, tell those sharing that they are welcome to stop and wait until the waitstaff has left. Don't be afraid if people shed tears, or if you do.

Intimacy Dinners are a time for real peer engagement and depth of understanding, not just current happenings, but of what experiences got us here and drive where we are going.

THE PHOENIX TRANSFORMED

In six months, PhoenixDX transformed. In the software development industry it is common for engineers and technical professionals to feel comfortable behind a computer. But consistent use of teamship practices like Sweet and Sour and the Personal Professional Check-in helped the team to realize that there was a group of humans in the room, not a group of job titles. That made a big difference to how they saw each other and collaborated. If the diagnostic assessment showed 2.4 at the start of the coaching journey, it now indicated 4.7 out of 5 for team bonding. "There's an amazing vibe, a really solid sense of connection and loyalty within the team," says Carrilho. "There's a collectivism in PhoenixDX that we are in this together; a sense of the value of shared ownership is lived through and through which was achieved by implementing in meetings and project teams the teamship practices as a new way of connecting and working." The software delivery and developer teams now relish the challenge of taking on mission-critical client projects together and they see each new project as a positive challenge to their professional development. (We will learn more about peer-to-peer development in chapter 10.) "There's a growth mindset on the consulting and delivery side because we have to adapt to many industries, many verticals, many different thinking styles from a customer perspective, and levels of customer maturity with technology," says Carrilho. "You build and find different ways of working with all of them. Aligning delivery with different customers requires flexibility, which is very important to us." And candor? Team bonding enabled much more candid conversations they would not have had otherwise. The developers realized that honesty is critical to ensure the success of the business—it isn't stepping on toes, it is really just speaking the truth so that the team can be the best that they can be.

Following the purposeful adoption of the teamship practices, PhoenixDX's rapid growth continues. But it's also now ranked as one of Australia's "Great Places to Work" and records a 4 percent annual staff turnover rate (compared to a 20–25 percent industry average where competition to retain talent is fierce). Founders Carrilho and Martin describe the culture of the business as "missionaries, not mercenaries," with trust as a core value. Carrilho says, "We trust our people to do the right thing—we've got their backs, they've got ours." It's Co-elevation in action and it's rooted in purposeful team bonding.

BUILDING A TEAM OUT OF A CRISIS

So much of this book is about aspirational challenge—about rising to the challenge of transformation and growth. But there are times when organizations face crises awful in their human consequences and which pose fundamental questions about teamship. One example is Pacific Gas & Electric (PG&E). How do you rebuild a team after a catastrophic organizational failure that led to the absolute devastation of a community and the deaths of eighty-five people in the Camp Fire blaze, which engulfed the town of Paradise in Northern California. The fire was caused by a PG&E high-voltage transmission line that broke loose from a nearly one-hundred-year-old tower in a forested area. The company pleaded guilty to eighty-four felony counts of involuntary manslaughter and reached a $13.5 billion settlement with victims and families, state and local agencies, and insurance companies, and declared bankruptcy in 2019 (exiting the following year). Experienced energy industry leader Patti Poppe was brought in as the new CEO in 2021 with a bold public safety pledge to bury ten thousand miles of power lines to reduce the future risk of wildfires. But Poppe brought a bold internal ethos too: to "lead with love"—to put humanity, empathy, and relationships at the heart of PG&E operational culture. In her first week, the brand-new leadership team gathered at the Claremont Hotel in Oakland for the first time. They took part in an exercise where each one charts their life as a river and maps the key life events on it. "Everyone stood up and poured their hearts out to each other because we were just meeting," says Poppe. "We were about to take this massive challenge to turn around this devastated company and to make it something amazing. There were tears as people were telling their stories and we got inside each other's hearts instantly." Only three members of the team had been with PG&E through the Camp Fire tragedy. "They told their stories. They had to help us understand what the organization had been through. And they each told their stories, how they had been around Paradise and listened to the 911 tapes, and why they were still at this company because they were committed to stay to make things right from the inside."

Starting with that investment in bonding helped to galvanize the team for the task ahead and created a foundation of empathy among peers. But it was not a one-and-done exercise. The commitment to team relationships and "leading with love" has been operationalized at PG&E through regular measurement of "team affinity." Poppe says, "We know that affinity, or care for one another, is essential to delivering extraordinary outcomes. It creates an environment in which people feel loved and cared for and safe, to perform, to try, to fail, to win, to succeed together. Part of building affinity is understanding a whole human and the things happening outside of work really do matter." Poppe's leadership team spends two Thursdays each month on meetings dedicated to affinity and relationships. "It's when we can go deeper," Poppe says. "Forming those bonds and giving people space to talk about what's happening in their life. And where do they need us? And how are they doing? And what have they accomplished?"

FROM PURPOSEFUL BONDING TO BUILDING RESULTS

Since the new team was formed, PG&E's investment in technologies and tools to reduce the risk of fires has topped $23 billion. That includes AI-powered cameras and drones to monitor equipment and new risk-monitoring systems. In 2023, six hundred miles of cables will be laid underground. For Poppe, it's a story of how an organization can shift from devastation to renewal. The future can be something other than the past. Poppe says, "It's really creating faith and a team of people to believe that we don't have to be what we were, that we can be entirely something else." It's a story of purposeful bonding, but it also invites us to consider the subject of our next chapter, team resilience.

CHAPTER 5

SHIFTING FROM INDIVIDUAL TO TEAM RESILIENCE

Red Flag Rule:
We lift each other up.

There is a "magic sauce" of team resilience, says Fran Katsoudas, the executive vice president and Chief People, Policy & Purpose Officer of Cisco. It is the shared understanding of everyone's highs and lows—the shift from resilience being your own burden to being a team sport. When I caught up with Katsoudas and Cisco's CEO, Chuck Robbins, and asked them how Cisco built team resilience, they described a range of very purposeful ways of working together. For the Cisco team, it starts with calling for increased awareness within the team and driving members to read obvious warning signs of a coworker struggling: someone consistently turning off video on calls or a marked decline in contributions to the discussion. Then there are formal practices that grow a heightened concern for each other's well-being as an ongoing team habit (we will explore those in this chapter's teamship practices). But running through everything Katsoudas and Robbins described is a common theme: resilience is about a team's ability to sustain the energy we all have for the work and commitment to support each other's mental and emotional well-being. To get there, the team needs to move from the traditional belief of "I know everybody's got enough on their shoulders, and I don't want to bother them with my stress" to the Co-elevation belief of "We own lifting each other up and sustaining each other through challenging times."

HOW A ROCKED PHARMACO SALES TEAM LIFTED EACH OTHER UP

After the dust settled from the restructuring, this formerly winning and proud 100+ sales team was down to little more than a dozen. The remainder were told to each take on much bigger sales territories that spanned multiple states and shift to a remote-first rather than high-touch face-to-face relationship-building model that they had developed over years, making them successful and differentiated with clients. "We felt abandoned. It was like the company"—we will call it PharmaCo—"wasn't invested in the success of the sales organization any longer," said Mali, one member of the team who had thought herself a star just a year before. "It was a total curveball." Stress was running high, partly because everything seemed to be ten times harder than needed. Hardest of all? Managing the expectations of existing clients who were used to a more personal touch. For the first time that any of the sales team could remember, they were not going to deliver the expected 5 percent sales growth.

"The approach of the previous management was kind of 'Okay, okay, you've aired your grievances, can we get on and hit the sales targets now?'" says Zara, who was brought in to lead the newly formed division. "I knew there was no way this team could get functional again until we heard and healed and then built toward a new winning collective culture. One that made each of them feel they had each other's backs." Zara created peer-to-peer forums for the team to address the practical problems they were all facing. "Not only did it make them feel heard in a productive manner, but we were finally able to start logging wins that lifted our energy," says Zara. Her objective was to form a self-supportive team that could shift from a negative spiral to a group responsible for each other's positive trajectory. At first, Zara's role in each meeting was only to encourage the team to look for solutions to their issues and stay constructive and forward focused. Soon the team of sales reps took ownership of the agenda. They determined what practical problems they needed help with—technical, logistical, and developing relational master classes to help manage new clients remotely—and created an agenda of troubleshooting workshops. But the team also went beyond giving each other professional support with common problems. With a little effort at the beginning from Zara, the team became bonded personally, using the teamship practices described in the last chapter, and explicit statements from Zara like, "You know, if we have each other's backs and take care of each other, this turnaround could not only be successful but more joyful." And that is exactly what the team decided to do. One member told me: "There were early instances where teammates had gone on medical leave and despite everyone's overload, others stepped in to cover their territory for them, which was exciting to show how we all could step up for each other. We struggled to do our new enlarged roles, but we leaned into finding energy for each other. We had team members with sick children who needed time off and the team stepped in. We found ways to do even more with so much less and it gave us energy to behave in this way." What used to be in-person support at the office turned into everyday phone calls, video calls, and text messages, but the team made sure that no one struggled alone. Did they hit their 5 percent sales target? They smashed it: 10 percent.

UNDERSTANDING TEAM RESILIENCE

A commitment to team resilience is a rare feature of any team's behavior. Before the coronavirus pandemic, our data suggested only 14 percent of team members felt they had a collective responsibility to lift each other's energy and a responsibility for each other's mental well-being. And most teams still treat resilience as an individual responsibility. Job-related stress negatively affects the mental health of more than 65 percent of workers, according to BetterUp, while work-related pressure adversely affects another 60 percent. Too often, such problems have been dismissed as indicating a lack of requisite toughness. There are several obvious diagnostic cues for leaders to identify stressors on team resilience. For example, performance: Are KPIs or OKRs being hit? There are few better diagnostics of whether something is going wrong. And resourcefulness: Is the team co-creating solutions or wasting time struggling to overcome problems? But the pandemic forced leaders to reconsider the centrality of mental health to productivity and other positive business outcomes. And even after the physical health crisis receded, the lessons about mental well-being's importance continue. We now know, for example, that every dollar employers spend on supporting mental health brings back a $4 return—higher productivity and lower absenteeism. We all saw glimpses during the pandemic of what it can be like when teammates and leaders share openly about struggles and mental health. Our research shows this as a great instance of where we should not go back to old work mindsets. Instead we need to leverage the collective humanity that arose at that time—even while everyone was working remotely—and go forward to work with a new, purposefully engineered, and more substantial commitment to greater transparency, less shame, and mutual care. World-class teams see resilience sustained, while average companies battle with flexible work policies and growing distrust. We need to reembrace resilience as a team discipline and encourage it. And it's the team's job to tease that out before it becomes chronic. It's the team's job to lift each other up.

TEAMSHIP PRACTICES

After completing the diagnostic and establishing the Red Flag Rule, two teamship practices support the shift from individual to team resilience:

1. **Energy Check-in:** A routine check at the beginning of team meetings to ask team members how they are feeling—and put a number on it.
2. **Resilience Spot Check:** A monthly deeper dive into how the team as a whole is feeling by looking into topics shown by research to erode resilience.

The Team Resilience Diagnostic

STEP ONE: *Team Discussion on Resilience*
Do teammates know where each other is struggling? And do they feel the duty that comes with Co-elevation to not only

care enough about each other to find out but to have responsibility to help?

It's a simple challenge of asking, *Do you know, do you care, do you act?* For most teams, the answer is no; they feel it's not their responsibility or perhaps believe it to be a private matter on which they should not impose. Our data shows that the typical team scores 1.9 on the 5-point scale, while a world-class team scores 4.5. The starting point for most teams is the old belief that resilience is down to individuals and perhaps HR—the diagnostic is the starting point for a discussion about shifting to address resilience together as peers, to understanding that it can be a team sport.

STEP TWO: *Diagnostic Question*
All team members give a score of 1 to 5 for the following question (1: Strongly disagree, 2: Disagree, 3: Neutral, 4: Agree, 5: Strongly agree):

➤   All team members feel responsible to lift each other's energy.

The diagnostic must be administered by a team member who is seen as agnostic and trusted, as the scoring is private and will not be attributed to individuals. Use an online survey tool or the Diagnostic Assessment on my website.

Red Flag Rule and Red Flag Replays
The simple Red Flag Rule for team behavior for team resilience is: "We lift each other up." Calling for a Red Flag Replay on this

particular shift within a month of practicing the below teamship practices and then regularly thereafter is an opportunity to hold space to talk about where things may have gone off the rails, to check that our new behavioral commitments are being observed and teamship practices are being implemented.

Teamship Practice: Energy Check-in

"To lift each other up, you must know where you're starting from," says Katsoudas. It's part of a simple but effective practice called an Energy Check-in. We ask teams this question at the start of a meeting: Where is your energy today on a scale of 0–5, and why? Zero means "I'm in the dirt," and five means "I'm skipping on rainbows with unicorns." This practice creates a formal and regular space for the team to share openly and vulnerably what they might be struggling with professionally or personally—and to put a number to it. An Energy Check-in is a safety net that is intentional, rather than leaving checking in with each other to chance encounters in the hallway or cafeteria. With this routine, concerted interest in others is a full team commitment rather than relying on existing friendship groups, who may or may not have this natural level of sharing. This deliberate teamship practice, coupled with the awareness that it's our responsibility to help one another, which is established with the new contract, assures the entire team develops shared empathy and then can be supportive of each other, and ensures transparency about where people are. It typically takes five to ten minutes for the group to share authentically and provides a safety net to catch those who have had challenging or even traumatic events in their professional or personal lives or are just at a point of exhaustion, in need of a lighter load. The combination of the new social contract—the team's agreement to have each other's backs—and this simple practice will show a real shift in team empathy and relationship scores from the original diagnostic benchmark. As everyone takes on the job of checking in with each other, they share ownership of each other's energy and well-being rather than leaving it to the leader's responsibility.

There's an added value to putting a number to how people are feeling, as Katsoudas explains. Let's take the example of one of the Cisco team, Tim. Tim never hits the five out of five on the energy scale. Every day he lives around three out of five. Sounds like a red flag. "Knowing that Tim is normally three out of five creates a space for him to be his authentic self; there's no pretending that he has to be a five," says Katsoudas. "I have a whole host of people who will say they feel like five. But if Tim ever feels like a four, it's something we'll celebrate." What Katsoudas at Cisco proves is that you can meaningfully track team energy levels, something many leaders would think is too tough to measure, let alone manage. Recording a simple weekly Energy Check-in provides an understanding of team well-being from a baseline reference point. It's an indicator of resilience. And if that Energy Check-in is shared in an open forum—in a team meeting—it's a prompt for peer-to-peer support if someone drops below their baseline or a cue for the celebration practices we will encounter in chapter 8 if, for example, Tim goes higher than that three.

Teamship Practice: Resilience Spot Check

I've been inspired by many conversations with Dr. Gabriella Rosen Kellerman, BetterUp's chief innovation officer and leader of BetterUp Labs, and her pioneering research, which features in the book she coauthored with psychologist and educator Dr. Martin Seligman, *Tomorrowmind: Thriving at Work with Resilience, Creativity, and Connection—Now and in an Uncertain Future.* Those conversations fueled my thinking about this teamship practice, a monthly check-in discussion with the team on a set of resilience factors to see where we are right now and how we are acting as a result. We ask the team only one question from the list below each month. For each question, each member of the team needs to give a score 0 (low) to 5 (high):

1. "Do I feel I'm on top of new ideas?" I've always rated my own cognitive agility as high—my ability to grasp new ideas and be ahead of the curve when it comes to understanding emerging concepts. But it's also a weakness in the sense that at times of stress, I don't always take the time and trouble to bring people along with me in the rush to get things done. It's a spot-check question for each member of the team.

2. "Do I feel like the work I am doing matters?" Research shows that purpose goes beyond mission statements; there is work, and there is the feeling that you—specifically you and no one else—are needed to do it. And if that work has meaning—a mission beyond making profits that resonates and is owned like a

grassroots movement within your organization—even better. But do you ever discuss that as a team?

3. "Do I feel like I'm ahead of the game in my area?" This is about the skill of foresight and planning for the future. In today's volatile environment, if the answer is no, how can the team help? In my last book, *Competing in the New World of Work*, I proposed that developing active foresight was a team task and developed a simple teamship practice for it.

4. "Am I still listening to my team?" As we saw in chapter 4, we need strong connections to flourish. Are we still listening to each other and our teams, or have we retreated into command and control? These questions, like the Energy Check-in, are questions to use to triangulate on items that research has proven to drive or erode resilience.

Each of these questions should create a discussion and bring up challenges and issues and opportunities for the team. From these discussions, threads of work can begin that may create Collaborative Problem-Solving questions—a teamship practice we will encounter in the next chapter—and along the way these threads of work could be brought back to the team for Stress Testing among the team. But the idea is to bring awareness to breakdowns in what we know are drivers and eroders of resilience and lead the team with individual members volunteering to help shepherd the work and take action.

WORKPLACES AS ENGINES FOR WELL-BEING

"We have the power to make workplaces engines for mental health and well-being," the US surgeon general, Vice Admiral Vivek Murthy, writes in the introductory letter to his *Framework for Workplace Mental Health & Well-Being*. But Dr. Murthy calls for us all to turn a "moment of crisis into a moment of progress." He says: "Doing so will require organizations to rethink how they protect workers from harm, foster a sense of connection among workers, show them that they matter, make space for their lives outside work, and support their long-term professional growth."

We have never felt more alone. More fractured. More fatigued. That's what makes teamship, the 10 shifts, and reengineering the way we work never more important, never more necessary.

CHAPTER 6

SHIFTING TO ELEVATE COLLABORATION: BROADER AND BOLDER CO-CREATION THROUGH MEETING SHIFTING

Red Flag Rule:
We co-create broadly to innovate boldly.

Red Flag Rule:
We leverage technology to elevate our collaboration.

When Matt Mullenweg opened his laptop, he showed me a glimpse into what 15 percent of the most disruptive companies know that the rest of us are barely awake to: a totally different way to engineer collaboration. There are a number of dynamics at play. The volatile times we live in demand bolder ideas and bigger thinking from all of us. We work in networks—not traditional, hierarchical org charts—that are pushing us to be broader in our collaboration and think beyond silos. We need to work faster, and more fluidly across borders and time zones. And meetings are not collaboration. Matt Mullenweg doesn't just know those things; he organizes his businesses around those collaborative dynamics. I caught up with the cofounder developer of WordPress—the open-source code used today by 43 percent of the web—and founder and chief executive officer of Automattic after our speaker sessions at Reid Hoffman's Masters of Scale Summit in San Francisco. He gave me an impromptu virtual behind-the-scenes look at how his team co-creates and innovates. "I call this an organizational blockchain," said Mullenweg, referring to his homegrown workflow and collaboration management system. "We've used this now for fourteen years. *Every* major decision, every design, every button, every pricing change, everything we have ever discussed and debated is here and it's permanent." He showed me how his company uses collaborative technology, where teams transparently share and critique ideas and solicit bold thinking and new ideas from broad-reaching constituents, all in an inviting format that looks uncannily like blog posts or a social media feed, complete with videos, images, links, and even GIFs. The code Mullenweg wrote at the age of nineteen changed the web and the world, so it's not a surprise he continues to leverage technology to engineer and transform their ways of working. His business has 1,900 employees working from more than ninety-three countries with no physical headquarters. As Mullenweg said, "We are a company that works on, and for, the web." Showing me the technology that supports his new ways of working, he said: "Whenever a new hire anywhere in the world needs to onboard into any collaboration and understand how we got here, we have a simple link for every debate we had and decision we made. And that will never change as long as the company exists. That's why I call it an organizational blockchain. It's a store of everything that's ever happened." Everyone's contribution to collaboration is valued. Nothing is lost. Nothing is wasted.

In our research with more than two thousand teams during the pandemic—the world's greatest universal inflection point for where we worked (shifting from office-based working to remote overnight)—we expected to find massive innovation around *how* we worked as well. Using our data, we created a five-point index of World-Class Digital-Forward Teams, Level One being teams struggling to leverage the digital basics and Level Five being digital dream teams. We were disappointed. As we've already mentioned, only 15 percent of teams had questioned and reinvented how they were working. Most teams were at Level One and Two: celebrating shifting meeting-based collaboration in offices to virtual video meetings—porting all the bad meeting room habits of meeting rooms to remote. But Level Four and Five digital-forward teams were using tools available to their fullest with functionality that improves traditional meeting-based collaboration along with software and ways of working for more effective communications and project and knowledge management. I was deeply inspired by leaders like Mullenweg, Drew Houston at Dropbox, and Rachel Romer at Guild Education who decided to use this inflection point to reconsider their ways of working. But these were not like the days when Mullenweg started WordPress and wrote code from his bedroom. Technology was much more advanced and so much was available for us to pick tools for our businesses off the shelf. Yet while leaders like Mullenweg, Houston, and Romer emerged as the new legends of ways of working, too many others thought they had achieved miracles by simply learning how to turn on and off a virtual meeting.

THE THIRD WAVE OF THE REINVENTION OF WORK

We're now in the third wave of the reinvention of work. If we look back in recent history to the changes of any significance that were made to ways of working, they were born from engineers. The first wave, in the 1980s and '90s, was Total Quality Management (TQM) and Six Sigma, born from engineers in manufacturing to improve quality in the face of daunting foreign competition. In the early 2000s, the second wave was Agile software engineering, which was created when the demand for software was outstripping capacity and a new system for working was needed. Today, when we need to reengineer the ways of white-collar working, where are the engineers doing this breakthrough work? CIOs, who were engineers, were clearly on the job to purchase new collaborative technology but didn't see it as their mandate to push for full adoption of those technologies. Instead, in a world that was grappling with a controversial question of how to "come back to work," we were looking at the problem from an HR policy perspective, not rethinking process and practice. As a reminder, our research showed that teamship was a combination of Co-elevating behaviors and practices along with new processes and tools. This chapter (along with the next chapter, where you'll read about candor and agile) is a rich source of these new teamship processes and tools.

In most nontechnology companies, where were the leaders like Mullenweg, Houston, and Romer who have put as much thought into reengineering their ways of working as they had into reinventing their disruptive unicorn business models? Unfortunately, at the time of this book's writing, the smartest minds of business have not yet turned to solving this problem, or even seeing the massive opportunity that exists to transform their way of working. This is precisely our mission: never to go *back* to work, but to go *forward* to work.

BROADER, BOLDER, MORE ADAPTABLE COLLABORATION

What Mullenweg showed me is an "untethering" of work in four ways:

1. **Teamship is untethered from the traditionally siloed org chart.** It is fully inclusive of those who should be involved to get to the boldest ideas fastest. One of the questions we'll ask in this chapter is "Who's your team?" We work in broad global networks inside and outside even the walls of our own companies, so we need to redefine how we think of "teams" and collaborate liberally outside the limited org chart. One of the answers is a teamship practice I'll describe later in this chapter called Teaming Out and the Relationship Action Plan (RAP), which helps to identify the right people, insight, and expertise we need beside and behind us to win. It's an idea I first raised in my book *Never Eat Alone* around building networks for opportunity in our lives. Years later I realized that leadership was nothing more than working effectively in networks inside of companies and I further developed the RAP for *Leading Without Authority*.

2. **Don't just adapt; embrace radical adaptability.** We cannot be reactive and conformist as a coping mechanism. We are predictive, proactive, and progressive and are radically adaptable because a volatile world demands that we be so. We cannot cling to old working habits and processes. We need to ratchet up our way of working and build systems to be more inclusive because we need more perspectives, more insight, more expertise, and more ideas, not less, because of the pressure of constant change. As I

wrote in my last book, *Competing in the New World of Work*, "Adaptability is a coping mechanism. Radical adaptability is a transformational mechanism." Through radical adaptability, you embrace the new world of work and grow with it, while others merely adjust and adapt to it.

3. **Go broad to go big.** In a world of constant disruption, we need bolder solutions. We need to untether from the fear of broader inclusion and embrace that broader collaboration does not lead to mushy consensus, it fuels us with the diversity of inputs to give us the bolder ideas we need. We will explore this even more in chapter 9, on embracing the power of diversity in our teams. It gets us faster to the innovation we need in today's volatile environment. Insight and ideas can be crowdsourced. Crowdsourcing allows organizations to cast a wider net to new ideas. And generative AI offers new potential to create personas—customers, experts, even competitors—to help stress-test ideas.

4. **Untether from meetings as the primary form of collaboration.** Traditional meetings are only one form of collaboration—and far from the best form or the most psychologically safe way to collaborate. As we will discuss later in the chapter, in-person meetings are great for dealing with particular team challenges, and as the final stage of collaboration to land the plane on a decision. But there are better forms of collaboration that are bolder, faster, and more

inclusive, such as asynchronous collaboration—people working to achieve the same goals but not at the same moment in time or in the same place. Whole cycles of collaboration can occur quickly—drawing in a broader team and stress-testing ideas—without a meeting needing to take place.

The last point shatters the myth of the meeting. Mullenweg is a zealot for listening to people—particularly the quietest voices in the organization. But except for board meetings, there are practically no standing meetings in his schedule. He is passionate about remote/distributed and asynchronous work—team collaboration that does not happen to live in real time. "There's a French term, *l'esprit de l'escalier*," said Mullenweg. "It means you've thought of the perfect witty reply to someone you've passed on the stairs when you've reached the bottom of the staircase. Guess what, that's sometimes how our minds work. It's like when you have a great idea in a shower or while you're walking around the block. But so much of how we work is optimized only for folks who are good at real-time conversation and in-the-moment brainstorming. One of the great things about distributed working is unlocking the genius of your introverts."

When world-class teams *do meet*, they use high-return practices like breakout rooms in remote sessions. In chapter 3, we heard about how breakout rooms can ignite candor, yet it's one of the most underutilized features of remote meetings. Remember that breakout rooms unlock the "Power of Three" to overcome the barrier that our research has revealed: in the average meeting of twelve people, only four people feel they are heard. Using breakout rooms and shared documents allows everyone to register their view. As we'll see when we run through this chapter's teamship practices, shared documents and breakout rooms help us to get the broadest perspective at the beginning of an initiative. Instead of someone calling a meeting with an already mostly baked assumption of the answer, we want to broadly span out and even ask people to contribute to the collaboration by saying candidly what they think the real problem is that we are trying to solve and then what they think the answer is. There would be no way to collect all that in a meeting. Now we are truly hearing each other. We're also using those contributions to figure out who should be in a meeting before a meeting even happens. Typically, we find that a number of people don't even need to be in the meeting. They just don't have a contribution to the final answer. Or they only need to participate in a subset of a bigger meeting. Again this saves us time in meetings. And the entire cycle of collaboration now happens in the cloud before the meeting, therefore shortening the collaboration cycle time by weeks, sometimes months. How many collaborations start with the meeting and just scratch the surface of the discussion, only to schedule several more meetings in the weeks and months to come without ever really getting to the mismatched understanding of the root cause and varied perspectives? Using all the tech tools at their disposal, world-class teams are reimagining collaboration to unlock faster and bolder co-creation.

A STORY OF TRANSFORMATION THROUGH BOLDER COLLABORATION

Eric Starkloff, the incoming CEO of NI (formerly National Instruments), was on a mission to reinvent the Texas-based automated test and measurement engineering firm. He wanted to speed up decision-making and accelerate growth. Starkloff believed the $1.2 billion company needed to become more agile—to operate more like a tech firm. He believed that culture change was required. He wanted his senior leaders to understand that they didn't always need to wait for him to make big calls. It was early 2020 and the COVID-19 pandemic was about to send the team remote. Fast-forward several months, and everything was different. The leadership team had engineered trust and created a culture of innovation and speedier decision-making. "The most tangible change is the ability to escalate and make critical business decisions faster," Starkloff says. "The process is co-creative, so the speed to execution is faster. We don't have to go do the old-school thing, seeking 'buy-in' which more than likely was not fully explored. In the past, we sometimes thought that collaborative decision-making and fast decision-making were at odds. But there are techniques for achieving both. It wasn't just a change in culture. It was a change in performance." Jason Green, NI's chief revenue officer and executive vice president for portfolio, highlighted how the effort to achieve goals broke through traditional silos. "The tangible outcome is increased sales and greater collaboration among the business units, with each seeing the others as empathetic allies," Green says.

ENLISTING PEERS WITHOUT LOSING AUTHORITY

Talking to Eric Starkloff about NI's transformation journey and his experience of our coaching process of a new social contract and teamship practices, he captured the fundamental shift of thinking that leaders need to make about broader and more inclusive team collaboration. "NI's leaders sometimes used to feel they had to take something on and figure it all out themselves," Starkloff says. "But you can enlist peers in the development of a solution without lessening your authority or accountability. It's a mindset: you don't have to solve that on your own." The transformation had been ignited by embracing high-return practices geared for inclusion, co-creation, and collaboration. It is the shift to creating value from interdependencies without impediment from hierarchies, traditional structures, or leadership hierarchies.

INTRODUCING THE COLLABORATION STACK

Ultimately, world-class teams think of collaboration not as a meeting but as a Collaboration Stack—four different modes of collaboration, each of which must be purpose-fully engineered.

1. **Asynchronous:** Teams collaborating on the same goals but in their own time and typically using collaborative technologies and shared documents instead of meeting
2. **Remote:** Real-time (synchronous) collaboration but with teams working remotely
3. **Hybrid:** Collaboration in real time but some people working remotely, some people in person
4. **In-Person:** Real-time collaboration where everyone is colocated

At the top of the Stack—the prerequisite for the rest, and in direst need of adoption—is asynchronous collaboration. Asynchronous promotes more productive workflows, but not with peers in the same meeting simultaneously. It allows for richer inclusion that fuels bolder innovation by permitting more people to engage in the topic with a level of freedom most can't feel in a meeting, without slowing the process down.

THE PURPOSE OF IN-PERSON MEETINGS

But it's not synchronous versus asynchronous. It is the strategic use of asynchronous and synchronous to create the optimal experience of both. Drew Houston told me that even though Dropbox has a policy of being remote first, *it's not remote only*. He believes in convening a good mix of in-person quarterly meetings for deeper team bonding. But in many companies, the development of asynchronous work is essential, and it must be a priority as part of a larger vision and strategy for work and collaboration. We can construct better, more focused meetings with just the right people in them or avoid meeting altogether. We need high-quality synchronous work with great in-person, hybrid, and all-remote meetings. There are times when colocated work is important. When we're physical, we should be engineering toward the emotional side of work: tough collaborations, bringing things to a conclusion among a tight group, celebration, play, bonding, connectedness, and gritty issues that are frustrating people and need to be wrestled to the ground with empathy. It kills me to see teams coming together and not leveraging the precious time together for what we do best in person. All of these make up the Collaboration Stack. Each stage of the Stack has unique attributes: each demands that you adopt and adapt teamship practices. Collaboration is not a meeting—it's a complex set of relational dynamics that, if you've cracked the code as our years of applied research have done, can ignite performance and accelerate growth.

A NEW MOVEMENT FOR NEW WAYS OF WORKING

Not tapping into everyone's perspective is a subpar result. Diversity of inputs and broader inclusion are powerful for getting bolder ideas, which we need for disruptive innovation, and for creating moonshots. As we said before, we don't need to go as far as Mullenweg and build a bespoke platform. Technology, like Google Workspace with its stack of apps, Docs, Sheets, Slides, Forms, and Chat, has made that broader and inclusive collaboration more accessible than ever before, opening up ways to Meeting Shift (see the teamship practice below)—to shift whole cycles of collaboration out of meetings to work with our collaborators asynchronously and accelerate the process of innovation. When I spoke to Microsoft CEO Satya Nadella, he was clear that we needed greater evangelization of new ways of working in the enterprise—we have great technology but have barely touched its potential. We need a new movement in the workplace for new ways of working; new advocates for embracing how technology can revolutionize remote work and the new potential of generative and agentic artificial intelligence.

FROM REMOTE AND HYBRID RESEARCH TO THE AI REVOLUTION: HOW NEW TOOLS ARE ENABLING THE TRANSFORMATION OF WORK

In 2012, we began research on remote work and designed a new suite of teamship practices around the core attributes of high-performing hybrid teams. We shared our findings and the interventions for hybrid teams in the *Harvard Business Review* under the banner "New People Rules in a Virtual World." Then the 2020 pandemic became the Great Laboratory for remote work—an opportunity to see the impact of our high-return remote and hybrid practices at scale. For those who applied the teamship practices, we tracked a three-to-fourfold lift in the key indicators of team performance: accountability and outcomes. In the years that followed, and long before the excitement that greeted the launch of ChatGPT in late 2022, our research extended to artificial intelligence in partnership with my friend the futurist Peter Diamandis, who said five years ago, "If your business is not driven by AI in the near future, you will be out of business."

When you are writing a book in the middle of an AI revolution, clearly what you write about AI and its impact on our teams will be moot by the end of the year. Yet, what we know is:

1. AI and humans will be coupled as teammates and AI will augment most of what we do. The transformation of work around AI has the promise of lowering costs, which is where a lot of people are looking at the problem today. But it also has the potential to elevate the sense of purpose and human connection that people have with their work. Success will be our ability to harmonize humans and AI to achieve both business objectives and human fulfillment at scale.

2. Value creation will become easier with fewer people as agentic AI develops, needing hardly any human supervision, and fewer and fewer people can do more and more with their AI counterparts. When Google

bought YouTube in 2006 it was shocking to see a billion-dollar valuation created by ten people. We will soon see a billion-dollar company created by one person and likely soon even one created by AI without human intervention. But this point just emphasizes the fact that we will be co-creating with AI as teammates, creating as much value as hundreds or thousands of former associates. In one sense, the concept of "teammate" will take on a whole new perspective. But not really. It's about how we co-create with other personas, be they human or AI.

As I write, we're seeing a great deal of fervor about AI yet a lack of broad and meaningful adoption. The reason for the hesitation to adopt generative AI is that our relationship with it is not the same as it was with traditional software. Software is a tool, while AI is a partner, and soon that partner will be thinking ahead of us and challenging us in powerful ways to think differently. Despite AI's potential to transform how we work, we're also seeing slower adoption and deployment because of workers' misplaced fear. Big lofty promises have made the tech intimidating. And it's made worse when AI sounds like Einstein is moving into your office. That will happen eventually, but today, the reality is closer to having an army of thousands of multiskilled associates on hand ready to execute at speed and scale exactly what you need to do. And like any intern, it just takes time to give that kind of direction—and you've got to give very specific directions (at least today, not tomorrow). But imagine what you can do:

1. Draw different kinds of expertise and insight into your team that you don't already have present. If you're a CPG company, developing a new product, you could use AI to gauge how different consumer personas might react. Let's say you're a B2B company and you're coming up with a new solution. You can stress-test it with a well-designed prompt that asks, How would a particular industry segment respond? The AI can represent "the voice of a competitor" in the discussion about strategy. As deep and broad as your curiosity is, you can train the AI to support it.

2. There is then a question of how AI can make your team more administratively effective. This could be as simple as calendar synchronization and automation of basic administrative tasks, from crafting emails to creating first drafts of documents. Soon, allowing the right people to engage around the right problems will be near instantaneous, save months of collaborative time, and allow us to reach thousands of just the right people with the breakthrough insights.

3. Team development and coaching will soon be augmented exponentially: With AI deeply embedded in our work, there is a mass of data around our individual performance to be gleaned that could aid our learning and skill development, productivity and effectiveness. How effective is our communication? Are we talking over people in meetings? Are our messages being misunderstood? If AI understands from our preparatory notes to a meeting what our perspective is,

why did we not raise a critical point at a key moment? If that's not available to us today, it's coming, and it will boost individual team effectiveness.

As I write these last points, I know they are too tactical, too short-term, and in future editions of the book, they will be removed as out-of-date. But for right now, it's where we are, and the era of AI-augmented teams is already leaving some organizations behind. As we said in the very first chapter, the shift from leadership to teamship demands a combination of new Co-elevating behaviors, new collaborative processes, and new tools. AI is more than a tool, it is a collaborator, a new member of the team that demands a reengineering of how we work for us to take advantage of its power.

TEAMSHIP PRACTICES

After completing the diagnostic and establishing the two Red Flag Rules, six teamship practices support the shift to elevate collaboration:

1. **Teaming Out and the Relationship Action Plan:** Who do we need to get the job done and how can we recognize that the broader our reach-out, the more innovative and bolder our answers might be?
2. **Asynchronous Stress Testing:** How to take the candor and P2P accountability teamship practice we

encountered in chapter 3 and turn it into a practice for unbounded collaboration, with no limits on who or how many people we can invite in to offer insight.

3. **Async Collaborative Problem-Solving (CPS):** Take an open-ended but business-critical question and use this practice to ignite inclusive collaboration.

4. **The Decision Board:** This teamship practice is a turbocharged version of Collaborative Problem-Solving; rather than one question, it takes a set of questions that need to be resolved in advance of a meeting.

5. **Calendar Bankruptcy:** This teamship practice is a sweeping review of schedules to eliminate unnecessary meetings.

6. **Scheduling Async Prep:** The adoption of async collaboration demands rethinking how you schedule time. This teamship practice is about how you make rich time in your calendar for prep.

The Collaboration Diagnostic

STEP ONE: *Team Discussion on Elevating Collaboration*
Is there a boundless spirit of co-creation within the team that drives toward innovation? Are we excited to look outside our org charts to find others to engage collaboratively to get the best and most inspired answers? Is the team making full use of all collaborative technologies and their features to accelerate their collaboration? These are the standards that world-class teams strive for and in our diagnostic exercise, they typically

achieve scores of 4.3 out of 5. In teamship, we leverage the great minds of the broadest definition of *team* to advance and sharpen and move our innovation bolder forward. We redefine *team* as not just those who work for us but those who can give us the best answers to breakthrough. But this boundless spirit of co-creation is rare. Our data shows that most teams score 2.5 out of 5 in our diagnostic exercise.

STEP TWO: *Diagnostic Questions*
All team members give a score of 1 to 5 for the following questions (1: Strongly disagree, 2: Disagree, 3: Neutral, 4: Agree, 5: Strongly agree):

➤ This team creates significant, tangible value from the interdependencies that exist between us.
➤ We are not impeded by hierarchy or a reliance on positional authority.
➤ This team crosses the finish line together, and we do whatever it takes to deliver on every aspect of the team's collective performance.
➤ All team members follow through on their own individual commitments and hold themselves accountable for their outcomes.
➤ Meetings are welcome and productive because we use them sparingly and as a complement with the most modern collaborative and AI tools that save us time and allow us to engage inclusively.
➤ We are inclusive and invite the broadest diverse set of opinions to find the most innovative solutions.

The diagnostic must be administered by a team member who is seen as agnostic and trusted, as the scoring is private and will not be attributed to individuals. Use an online survey tool or the Diagnostic Assessment on my website.

Red Flag Rules and Red Flag Replays

The two teamship Red Flag Rules for collaboration: "We co-create broadly to innovate boldly" and "We leverage technology to elevate our collaboration." Calling for a Red Flag Replay on this particular shift within a month of practicing the below teamship practices and then regularly thereafter is an opportunity to hold space to talk about where things may have gone off the rails, to check that our new behavioral commitments are being observed and teamship practices are being implemented.

Teamship Practice: Teaming Out and the Relationship Action Plan

Most of us think of our teams as the people who report to us. But the reality is that that is an old way of thinking about work. Who do we need to get the job done and how can we recognize that the broader our reach-out, the more innovative and bolder our answers might be? It doesn't matter if people are inside or outside the organization. As the person who wrote the bestselling book on networking *Never Eat Alone*, over time I applied that research and insights to learning how to work and lead most effectively in networks. You can talk about what you have to do and where you're going, but you need to start introducing who makes up your team and who are the people you need to build relationships with to achieve your goals. And that's Teaming Out. To Team Out you need to build a Relationship Action Plan (RAP). The RAP requires you to capture in a shared doc:

1. Identify the most critical relationships to each goal success. Also recognize these are not just those you need to get buy-in from, they are your team. Full stop. You need to co-create with them and serve, share, and care and have a social contract with them. Teaming out means that each goal you have has a relevant team associated with that goal.

2. Measure your progress enlisting them. Use a scale of minus 1 to 5.

   −1 = it's a strained relationship

   0 = they don't know about or care about our work

   1 = they are aware but not really engaged

   2 = they are engaged lightly, not really collaborating deeply

   3 = they are collaborating and engaging regularly

   4 = they are advocates and offering innovation and really stepping forward to offer risks and challenges

   5 = they are true ambassadors, totally under the tent with us and driving the recruitment of other important teammates

   It's then essential to prioritize who are your most important teammates with an ABC.

   A = the core day-to-day constant working team

   B = those you will gain the most from and who can hold

the progress back the most. We want to co-create with them and really engage in the team—that may not happen in day-to-day stand-ups but will occur in the regular sprint reviews, which we will learn more about in our next chapter on agile teams.

C = influencers that we need to be engaged with at some level. These individuals may only be involved for Stress Testing at the key project milestones.

So now you've got two metrics: Relationship Quality (RQ) and Priority. It's critical that you move all the As to RQ 4 and 5; they are your core critical team after all, and you want them all to be deeply Co-elevating around your shared goals. Most of the Bs need to be at least RQ 3, 4, or 5. One key is not to spend too much time trying to convert the –1s but instead get real traction and results and that will help convert those –1s. We call that the Saul-to-Paul conversion— the biblical Road to Damascus moment when the persecutor of Christians became an apostle—when you get the naysayer swayed, but trying too early can just waste time and prevent you from ever getting traction.

3. Actively build and nurture. You can allocate individuals on the team targets to build relationships with. These could be contractors. They could be clients. They should be customers. Expand the list over time and monitor progress regularly, at least at the end of every month with the day-to-day team. Co-elevate with both customers and suppliers.

Avoid Needless Reorgs

Many enterprises chase the pendulum of organizational redesign because one part of the business and an adjacent part are not collaborating effectively. It's determined that we have to shift the span of control of one group or another. A couple of years later, there's another reorg because we're bumping into another problem at another adjacency of what one group wanted control over. And another few years we call in another consulting firm and they redesign the org chart, yet again. Sound at all familiar? Work is often described as existing in multiple dimensions: business P&Ls, support functions, geographies, etc. That may be a decent way to describe an organization but that's not *how work gets done*.

Our conceptualization of how work should be organized is that it needs to start with goals. Every goal has a team involved in achieving it. Who is on that team? That brings us back to the idea of Teaming Out and Relationship Action Plans and seeing teams consisting of the appropriate network, a multidisciplinary collaboration that is convened to achieve a goal. It's drawn from a network rather than a rigid org chart—with each multidisciplinary team executing goals in sprints of work (which we will discuss in the next chapter). I've always said to my clients, please don't rush into a reorg; let's first have a shot at coaching our team leaders how to lead across the organization through first getting clear on our goals and then designing inclusive RAPs and working these networked teams in agile sprints. In these cases, we are merely implementing agile teamship within a networked organization.

Teamship Practice: Asynchronous Stress Testing

In chapter 3, we introduced the Stress Test as a means to introduce more candor and peer accountability to the team. But Asynchronous Stress Testing is unbounded; there are no limits to who or how many people we can invite into our collaboration to find the most impactful answers to the challenges we are likely to face. This allows us to be more inclusive and embracing of diverse opinions than ever before. That's exactly what I found at a large auto manufacturer when a collaboration that started with fifteen people expanded thanks to Async Stress Testing, leading us to find a solution to a divisive item that had been holding them back for months. The final game-changing insight came from a person three layers removed from the original fifteen who would have never been invited to the discussion otherwise. And we can also stress-test our assumptions with diverse opinions prompted by AI. It is now easy to have various AI personas stress-test and challenge our ideas and assumptions as we curiously pursue broader insights and innovation than our limited core team may have.

For further clarity, let's imagine a leadership team who has been challenged by the CEO and CFO to find cost savings. In an upcoming meeting, the chief information officer is ready to present her proposal to cut costs, by centralizing what was previously distributed IT resources. The CIO was expecting some pushback from business unit leaders against the idea of more central control of IT and the loss of business unit customized attention. So, in true old-style meeting fashion, the CIO has already presold the package to the CFO, brought up many of the likely challenges with the CEO, and asked both for their backing before even coming into the room. At the meeting, the CIO opens the discussion among the team by presenting her proposal. The CIO's presentation is a standard "report out." Some of the business unit leaders can tell this has already been politically stitched up with the CFO and CEO and decide not to express their viable discontent over risks and concerns, as they feel it wouldn't matter if they did say anything. Some individuals have now decided to do their own lobbying later with the CEO, so will hold their arguments as not to get into an open debate, assuming a private hearing will advantage them more. Some are unwilling to make recommendations even though their gut tells them there is a better way to do this, as they have not had enough time to think it through thoroughly. As we'll learn more about in chapter 6, when there are twelve people in the room, only four voices are likely to be heard. Real candor is noticeably absent. There's an unspoken belief that it's best to move to the next agenda item for now, and try to deal with this outside the meeting. Welcome to an everyday meeting in corporate life anywhere in the world today. Now let me lay out a different scenario.

In this second scenario, the CEO has framed a North Star understanding that, under the current economic climate, there are cost constraints and a need to identify cost reductions. The CIO, in response, creates a quick one-pager in the following format:

➤ Here's what we know and have done already to figure out the best solution.

➤ Here's where we're struggling; there are challenges and knotty issues on this topic.

➤ Here's our plan for going forward as it stands today.

The one-pager, perhaps associated with a short video from her so everyone hears her tone appropriately on such sensitive issues, is shared either as a simple narrative document or a slide. In all cases, the one-pager is accompanied by a group editable spreadsheet with all twelve proposed meeting attendees named in the left-hand column. Along the top row, there are three simple questions for each member of the team to answer:

1. What challenges or risks do you see that we're missing?
2. What innovative/bold ideas or solutions do you have that could benefit the situation?
3. What help or support can you and your team provide to address this?

This is sent out at least a week before the meeting for all teammates to consider and respond, giving every contributor serious time to think, consult their teams, and answer those questions before the meeting . . . and then to read each other's answers. Knowing that, in the past, preparatory work before meetings was often not done, use of assigned names on a shared document increases the likelihood of completion because of open accountability among peers with the visibility of the CEO. What we've just done is Meeting Shifted, mov-

SHIFTING TO ELEVATE COLLABORATION

ing an entire cycle or multiple cycles of collaboration to before the meeting. The CIO can come into the room with an agenda that addresses concerns and poses a few gritty areas that would benefit from wrestling together as a group. But unlike the first scenario, which will drag on for weeks, maybe months, this allows the team to possibly finish in one meeting.

Other Asynchronous Collaboration Teamship Practices

With asynchronous preparation, all team members can thoughtfully write down what they want to say for everyone to read and comment on in advance. You've radically reduced the cycle time because you can go into the meeting discussing next steps since everyone has already been heard—they've written it down and it's been read in advance. A lot of people think that you can do a quick preread just before a meeting or do it in the first ten minutes of the meeting. But that misses out massively on the inclusion, because people haven't had time to thoughtfully read it and respond to the group in advance and to have everyone read each other's perspectives. Waiting to read the pre-work in the meeting skips an entire valuable cycle of collaboration and can elongate the cycle time of collaboration by weeks. Async Collaborative Problem-Solving and the Decision Board are two other practices that can supercharge your team's asynchronous preparation.

Async Collaborative Problem-Solving (CPS)

Asynchronous Collaborative Problem-Solving (CPS) focuses attention on a single business-critical question

that's relevant to an ongoing collaboration and perhaps
a forthcoming meeting—but definitely *before a meeting*.
Asynchronous CPS is for more open-ended, top-of-the-
funnel collaboration questions rather than Stress Testing,
which is focused on making an existing opinion or thread
of work better and more bulletproof. In my experience
as a coach, too many teams just avoid putting the most
important and difficult questions on the table to be
discussed and dealt with. Async is a great way to get these
out in the open from the broadest parts of the company and
team. It's also a big part of the social contract. We dare to
say what is most difficult to share. But we are committed
to the mission and each other. To align a team to their
North Star, the CPS can be aimed at bringing clarity and
transparency and alignment in on the following critical
areas:

> ➤ **North Star Mission:** Where are we misaligned
> around our mission as a team? Where are we
> misaligned around our priorities of getting there?
> ➤ **Goals:** What are the biggest hills we need to take to
> achieve success?
> ➤ **Priorities:** What are the 2–3 things we need to get
> greater traction on in the next three months?
> ➤ **Redundancies:** What do we have to stop doing in
> order to make room for the top priorities we have?
> ➤ **Risks:** What are the greatest challenges we will face
> in the next 3–6 months (or year)?
> ➤ **Transparency:** What topics or questions are most

important for us to address as a team that we are not addressing?

Any of these questions is accompanied by a Google Sheet or shared spreadsheet that lists the names of everyone attending and space for people to record their insight and answers before the meeting. It is encouraged that everyone draws in data or insight from their wider teams. One thing I often tell teams about the benefit of Async CPS and involving wider teams in advance is that, traditionally there is a live debate in the room that comes to a conclusion, but then later team members seem to backslide from their commitment. Sometimes this is a problem of candor and a lack of original commitment. But often it is because when team members have returned to their wider teams, they have been made aware of issues they were unaware of that put them in a new state of disagreement. This async process avoids that and ensures that all available data is clear up front so we can land the agreement once and for all. Google Docs and the ability to respond, resolve, and revisit comments stands as a permanent record or progress on a project—an audit trail of decision-making that can be retraced by the team and other teams in the future.

Once everyone has read everyone's input, they come to the meeting prepared to dive in. After everyone reads everyone's answers, there can be one more round of comments in a new column for each person to assist again in getting right to the point in the meeting. People can agree with others or share differences of opinion in the new column once they have read all their peers' comments. Then, just before the meeting, everyone reads all the final comments, and the leader of the meeting decides: 1) What is the agenda we actually need to land the plane? Sometimes the item has already been resolved. 2) Who *really* needs to be involved? Often it's a much smaller group that contributes to the reduction of meetings on all of our calendars, upward of 30 percent. 3) Or do we go straight to giving "Yes, No, Maybe" feedback to everyone? (*"Yes, we will do this,"* *"No, we won't do this for this reason,"* and *"Maybe, we will study this."*) Then we have the meeting to stress-test the final conclusions one more time and land the plane.

The Decision Board

The Decision Board is a supercharged variation of CPS and happens early in the collaborative process. The variation is that instead of a single CPS question, it's a set of questions that must be answered in advance. The idea is that any information presented for a decision in a meeting must start with either a prerecorded video or a simple write-up. That preparatory reading or recording is accompanied by a Google Sheet or shared spreadsheet that lists the names of everyone attending the meeting in one column and across the rows asks a series of critical questions related to the agenda item. In the automotive manufacturer referenced above, they were struggling over delays in their retooling of manufacturing that was required to meet commitments made to customers and investors. The set of simple but powerful questions asked was:

➤ What is the core problem we're trying to solve? (*Looking to ferret out any misalignment*)
➤ What are other bold solutions we should consider?
➤ Where will progress get stalled? (*Who or what inside the organization may have issues with the possible bold solutions?*)
➤ Who should be invited to this discussion? (*Who might contribute greater innovation? Who will be integral to execution? Whom would we benefit from listening to, even outside the organization?*)

Those who are assumed to have insight to the issue are asked to complete the form before any meetings are scheduled. The meeting agendas and those invited are ultimately derived from the input after an entire round of debate is had in these documents, which is more robust than if you were starting from cold in a meeting with no prep. In that case, it would take many meetings after to align on the problem and get to solutions over months that might be circumvented in just a couple of weeks.

Teamship Practice: Calendar Bankruptcy

We all know meetings are the world's most overabundant commodity. Data we have tracked since 2000 on the performance of high- versus low-performing teams shows that meetings have always been a broken forum for collaboration. Research across twenty industries by organizational psychologist Dr. Steven Rogelberg and Otter.ai shows that at least one in three meetings is unnecessary. And companies with

5,000 employees would save more than $100 million annually if those unnecessary meetings were dropped. Organizations with 100 workers would save almost $2.5 million per year. Calendar Bankruptcy is a sweeping review of diaries to eliminate unnecessary meetings. No agenda? Simply delete. No decision to be made? Delete that too. The Calendar Bankruptcy exercise echoes the new year schedule purge of Tobi Lütke, CEO of the e-commerce company Shopify. Lütke told his team in January 2023 to purge their calendars of all recurring meetings of more than two people. He encouraged his team to decline other meetings, exit large chat groups, and adhere to a No-Meetings-Wednesday policy. In total, 76,500 hours of pointless meetings were culled. Since then, Shopify has gone further and added a meetings-cost app to its calendar that tallies up the bill for a meeting based on the length of meeting and average cost of attendees. "No one at Shopify would expense a $500 dinner," according to Chief Operating Officer Kaz Nejatian. "But lots and lots of people spend way more than that in meetings without ever making a decision." Shopify joins companies like Dropbox that moved beyond the debate about where we work toward reengineering how work gets done.

Teamship Practice: Scheduling Async Prep

People often ask, "So how do we find time for all this new async pre-work? I barely have time for what I'm doing now." Scheduling async time on your calendar is as important as a meeting. For any time you need to spend doing async prep, creative thinking, review, or strategic thinking, you need to allocate time in your schedule specifically. We all know the alternative is that we end up with that time being shifted into nights or weekends otherwise, and it often does not get done. It's why we often attend meetings unprepared even though the preread has gone out in advance. Creating a distinct calendar entry for this time allows you to see the success you have moving this to work hours and allows you to see how much time it takes, which is significant. The successful use of this new collaborative system will save tons of time previously spent in meetings, as so many leaders have discovered. More importantly, it will give us richer and faster outcomes. You and your teammates will get better and better at estimating what it really takes to do all these things and who needs how much time for what. Some people take an hour to do the same thing, others take thirty minutes. And reporting back to those who sent the suggested prep how long it took (and, by the way, they need to tell you what they think it will take so you can schedule that time) can help them better tune the request from the start. We all get smarter for what this all takes. We need to honor async time just as much as, but not more than, meeting time.

WE NEED TO SHATTER THE MYTH OF THE MEETING

Every day there is a team somewhere making decisions without having heard the best and brightest ideas. Every day there is a team crowding out time in their schedules for strategic and creative thinking by adding . . . Yet. Another. Meeting. Our research shatters the long-believed myth that collaboration only happens in a meeting. Too many teams are teams toiling under this mistaken belief that if you include more people, you will be slowed down in your decisions and your outcomes will be diluted somehow—the more voices, the more noise, and for longer. It's simply not true. Our data shows there is very little proactive recognition that we now work in networks and that we should systematically work with external stakeholders who are critical to our success. Taking broader inputs into decision-making can create bolder and faster decision-making. Never before has it been so approachable as in an increasingly hybrid and remote world of work.

CHAPTER 7

SHIFTING TO AGILE AS THE NEW OPERATING SYSTEM FOR YOUR TEAM

Red Flag Rule:
Agile is our operating system.

BM lifers said it could never be done and it was crazy to try. But CEO Arvind Krishna set the audacious goal of abandoning IBM's forty-year sales divide between software and consulting and creating a new connected, simpler, and more effective go-to-market model—in six months. Krishna does not see organizational transformation as a long, slow process; like so many other leaders in this book, he is an engineer by training and an advocate of agile not only for software development but for the enterprise overall. "It's not the instinct of most executives to operate in agile because what has most likely made them successful and put them into senior positions is that they were able to progress and innovate by coming with a suggested outcome all packaged up with a bow around it and presenting it to the boss," says Krishna. "The very natural instinct is not to show the sausage-making. Agile celebrates when everyone can see what's not that pretty along the way." That's precisely what he asked the IBM executive team to do.

The go-to-market transformation would touch every aspect of IBM's operations, from finance to R&D to customer service. This wasn't just a sales project. The agile approach first saw multidisciplinary squads formed, drawing in talent across the business to tackle "big hills" that needed to be taken. This was not a project that could be done in silos. "We did biweekly stand-ups," says Rob Thomas, IBM's senior vice president for software and chief commercial officer. "I think this was a great demonstration of how very senior leaders could iterate and start at the very beginning with: *we know we have a problem; we probably have to get aligned to what problem we all think we have; it's okay that we have no idea how to solve it; but we're going to commit to be aligned around a process that we know will solve the problem.* Then the biweekly sessions became more about sharing real traction, identifying gaps, identifying what has to come next. *What have we achieved? What's been in the way? What do we need to do in two weeks?*"

Nickle LaMoreaux, IBM's chief human resources officer, who joined one of the agile squads, said the beauty of leveraging agile for this big mission was in breaking complex problems into manageable pieces and timelines. LaMoreaux says: "We're not in a conference room trying to solve world hunger as we have done in the past. We were breaking problems into hills, tangible clear hills with short timelines and diverse and very inclusive, relevant squads. It also makes it easier to recruit people to the squads. You don't have to be overwhelmed and worry about everything in six months. Let's talk right now about what we are going to do for large clients in our major markets, and once we have a vision for the end state, let's break that down into the next two to four weeks of work with clear outcomes focused on the customer." One output of the process was major and achieved organizational alignment around both sales team goals and the measurement of their performance—bringing a very new level of transparency. What was most important was that the new go-to-market plan succeeded and delivered sales growth. In 2022, IBM software revenues were up 12 percent, consulting up 15 percent, and infrastructure up 14 percent on the prior year. "When we talked to some former IBMers about the direction we were headed, to a T everybody said *this will be a massive failure—you guys are crazy, you have no idea what you're getting into*," says Thomas. "But sales accelerated through the process of the change. It wasn't even like there was a dip, and things came back. There was acceleration the whole way."

THE ORIGINS OF AGILE

When a small group of IT professionals drafted the original Agile Manifesto at a ski resort in Utah in 2001, they were responding to the world's growing impatient demand for software and the urgent need to dramatically accelerate slow, hierarchical, bureaucratic production and review processes that were making software redundant by the time coding was finished. Customers were being failed. Now enlightened leaders like Krishna at IBM are applying agile principles as a required operating system for modern work—not just software development—to meet the same impatient demands of today's volatile work environment. We can't keep approaching strategic change and transformation programs with the slow, hierarchical, command-and-control-style management of the past. Research shows that two out of three Fortune 500 companies have been forced to drop major strategic change programs. Yet despite so many companies having deep agile practices in their technology and engineering groups, relatively few leaders have used the agile principles at the team level. This is a big miss.

The exception was that, during the pandemic, we managed something extraordinary: all of us were agile out of necessity. We practiced what I call "crisis agile." With one of the largest airlines, we had been facilitating quarterly agile sprints aimed at fundamentally reinventing the travel industry. When the pandemic hit, they went to daily agile sprints to survive. Each day this executive team gathered and reflected on what they had been able to achieve the day before, where they were struggling, what they had learned, and what was new on any number of dimensions, and then with all that new information, they pivoted as needed and committed to what they were going to do tomorrow. In Detroit, a friend of mine from one large industrial automotive company said, "Crisis is when we are at our best." Indeed, we know that's when we develop heightened empathy and come together and bond more deeply. We collaborate more freely to figure things out. We empower each other and put hierarchy and silos aside. But as in all crises, the way we were doing it during the pandemic was fatiguing and unsustainable, which awakened the need for higher degrees of mental health focus and team resilience. The point is, by reinventing the process of how we work, we can actually be at our best: we can be radically adaptable but in a sustainable way that increases flexibility, collaboration, speed, and the ability to make transformation a normal everyday occurrence, a constant. This is the operating system to become dream teams.

KEEPING AGILE SIMPLE

For the 80 percent of the companies who try to adopt agile at scale, at some point they run into resistance because of the complexity and rigor of the agile process as it is often taught to full implementation. While that may not be an issue for the meticulous work of software or in detailed manufacturing project management, it is often raised when you try to apply agile across an enterprise. Agile can come in different flavors with different degrees of bureaucracy and terminology— tribes, squads, chapters, and guilds, for example. But we're going to let the adoption and curiosity of deeper levels of agile execution be up to those who gain success from what we're about to share and want more. For now, let's keep it simple and introduce a few key elements of agile that make any team more radically adaptable in today's volatile world.

TEAMSHIP PRACTICES

After completing the diagnostic and establishing the Red Flag Rule, seven teamship practices support the shift to agile as the new operating system for teamship:

1. **Creating a Customer-centric Agile Brief:** It's the starting point for agile teamship—what's the best solution for the customer?
2. **Sprints:** The key practice of breaking down complex projects into smaller, simpler sprints of work.
3. **Sprint Stress Testing:** Adding the Stress Test teamship practice we first encountered in chapter 3 to a sprint review at the end of a delivery cycle creates a challenge culture that you don't often see in traditional agile stand-ups.

4. **Async Agile Stress Testing:** Scheduling regular stand-ups can be challenging for global teams working across time zones. Sharing reports and documents asynchronously, as described in chapter 6, allows teams to stress test and offer candid feedback and support.

5. **Empowering Teams Between Sprints:** The time between sprints is an opportunity for candid conversations among the team about how to improve for the next delivery cycle.

6. **Foresight Five Minutes:** A simple monthly practice to help your organization constantly own the act of seeing around corners.

7. **Decision Governance:** Making great team decisions at speed requires a clear process when you want bold and inclusive collaboration across a networked organization—who will drive the process, who will be consulted, who will be informed, and who will make the final decision.

The Agile Diagnostic

STEP ONE: *Team Discussion on Agile as the New Operating System*

The awakening to being agile is whether we are breaking our work down into short powerful sprints, and then at the end of those two-week or one-month sprints, are we exposing our progress to the broadest members of our teams to ensure we are staying true to the North Star? Are we making amazing progress? Have we missed any risks or opportunities or market forces that have arisen or been seen by someone who could help us crush it and stay on track? Do we need to adapt and pivot to meet our objective? Do we measure our progress in outcomes and traction, not just on analysis or work done? Are we honest with ourselves and the public about where we are struggling to ask for help? Are we getting the broadest input to our progress and assumptions; are we truly Teaming Out and building our RAP and inviting in all A, B, and C priority teammates?

With Team Agile, the job of every team is to innovate and create greater and greater customer value, fast. Talking to Dr. Michael Ackerbauer, Business Transformation Leader at IBM, what works so well with the company's approach to agile is its simple three-principle approach:

1. Clarity of outcome
2. Iteration over perfection
3. Self-direction to unleash innovation

There are some really simple messages for leaders in this. We always need a North Star to look toward at the end of each sprint—a clear outcome. It's not about perfection, it's about being able to adapt and pivot toward our goal. Also, achieving Team Agile requires (allows) leaders to pull back from micromanaging operations and spend more time defining the intended outcomes and expectations that will drive their agile team's trade-offs and decisions. When done right, leading through Team Agile doesn't mean throwing away control. It means modernizing it.

STEP TWO: *Diagnostic Question*

All team members give a score of 1 to 5 for the following question (1: Strongly disagree, 2: Disagree, 3: Neutral, 4: Agree, 5: Strongly agree):

➤ We adopt agile principles in our work process and iteratively prioritize and adapt to new information and competing demands.

The diagnostic must be administered by a team member who is seen as agnostic and trusted, as the scoring is private and will not be attributed to individuals. Use an online survey tool or the Diagnostic Assessment on my website.

Red Flag Rule and Red Flag Replays

The simple Red Flag Rule for the shift to agile as the new operating system for teamship is: "Agile is our operating system." Calling for a Red Flag Replay on this particular shift within a month of practicing the below teamship practices and then regularly thereafter is an opportunity to hold space to talk about where things may have gone off the rails, to check that our new behavioral commitments are being observed and teamship practices are being implemented.

Teamship Practice: Creating a Customer-centric Agile Brief

The agile process starts and is sustained by a noble mission: the customer-centric problem that needs to be solved. Satisfying the customer was described in the first line of the original Agile Manifesto as "the highest priority." In Krishna's case, it was creating a consistent problem-solving approach across IBM's organization to customers' needs—not different approaches from different teams. Customer-centricity (whether an internal customer/stakeholder or external customer) creates alignment for the team for the duration of the project. It's the starting point and the North Star when there is a question about direction or next steps. Everyone wears the same hat: *What's the best solution for the customer?*

When creating a customer-centric brief, clarity of outcome is essential.

➤ What precisely are we trying to achieve for the customer?

➤ What are the measurable goals?

➤ What is the scope of the work?

➤ What are the timelines?

It's an obvious opportunity to draw on data but also the time to include marketing, sales, and customer support associates in the team, and for Stress Testing. Sounds simple, but everyone in a multidisciplinary team needs to understand who the end customers are, what problems they have, and what solutions best serve their needs right now. As some business functions have little engagement with customers, it may not be obvious or there may not be a coherent view across the whole enterprise. It's vital to create that clarity within the team at the outset: *Who do we serve? How can we serve them better?*

B2B organizations can go further. Critical relationships exist outside the business as well as within the organization, so deepening relationships with vendors and customer groups can provide sources of external information and insight that they had never directly engaged with before. Clients should be part of Teaming Out and our Relationship Action Plan. We can even invite actual customers to join in Stress Testing and gather valuable input and insight directly. It's obvious. We should draw customers into the team if our starting question as we form teams is goal-oriented and that goal is customer-centric.

Teamship Practice: Sprints

If the first step of IBM's three-principle approach to agile was clarity of outcome and creating a clear brief, the second was iteration over perfection. The key practice of successful agile is breaking down a complex marathon project that could last many months into smaller, simpler, less daunting sprints of work lasting two weeks to a month, depending on the work that needs to be done within that sprint. This also assures that there are regular inclusive Stress Tests and necessary adjustments along the way so the guarantees of staying on course to the projected outcomes are more assured. Successful sprints have these common characteristics:

1. **A great brief.** Without the initial Customer-centric Agile Brief described above, there is no North Star for the team to follow. Creating the brief is the firing pistol on "sprint zero" when the multidisciplinary

team can stress-test a brief's working assumptions to have absolute clarity about what is going to be delivered, by whom, and when.

2. **Ruthless prioritization.** There's a difference between what's urgent, what's important, and what's both! Being able to focus attention on the most pressing and high-value tasks that make up the sprint is the key attribute in the most successful agile teams.

3. **Keep moving forward.** Quick-fire "stand-up" meetings—daily if necessary but as often as the pace of change requires—during the sprint can keep the team always moving forward. Stand-ups are short with the aim of checking if priorities have changed, or if there is a need to pivot in a new direction— willingness to change (even at a late stage of a project) being an essential agile principle. Daily stand-ups typically ask three customer-centric questions from each member of the team:

➤ What value creation did I contribute since we last convened?
➤ What value creation am I working on today?
➤ Where do I need help to ensure I am maximizing value creation?

This quick update aims to see team members self-assign tasks (self-assignment of tasks being the third of IBM's basic agile principles), identify any roadblocks, and allocate support.

4. **Sprint Reviews.** At the end of the delivery cycle, stakeholders need to review progress against the original plan. At the heart of the sprint review is a Stress Test, the next teamship practice.

Teamship Practice: Sprint Stress Testing

Many years ago when I first came across the agile methodology, I borrowed from the idea of stand-ups—of people saying, "Here's what I've done, here's where I'm struggling/what I learned, and here is where I'm planning on going next"—and inserted that into Stress Testing, the practice we first encountered in chapter 3. But the difference between a stand-up *during a sprint* and Stress Testing *in a sprint review at the end* is that the stand-up is just among the agile team and the Stress Test happens at a delivery milestone among all stakeholders. The key people in validating the Stress Test and how much has been achieved in the delivery cycle are, of course, the customers themselves or their proxy. By adding Stress Testing to a sprint review at the end of a delivery cycle, we're extracting a high degree of challenge culture and the courage to give candid feedback that you don't often see in stand-ups.

Teamship Practice: Async Agile Stress Testing

One large industrial manufacturer of CPG products had been committed to agile for many years, but for a global business, they found it was challenging to schedule regular stand-ups for teams across many time zones. They adopted

Asynchronous Stress Testing, described in chapter 6. This allowed each sprint leader to distribute a video report to everyone in the team—and wider stakeholders—along with a Google Doc for challenges and offers of support to get much more candid feedback remotely over the next day, accommodating people's time zones.

There is an added benefit of Stress Testing in sprint reviews at the end of the delivery cycle. If the Stress Test is carried out asynchronously and shared with stakeholders beyond the multidisciplinary team working on the project, there is an opportunity for distributed learning, knowledge transfer, and greater alignment. Lessons, ideas, and issues that have been encountered and overcome by the team are shared more widely in the organization rather than just contained within the team. This is a simple way of sharing knowledge and gaining alignment within an organizational matrix.

Teamship Practice: Empowering Teams Between Sprints

What did the team learn during the sprint? If we look at what we did versus the goal and what the customer needs, what would we do differently next time? Are we doing the right work? What didn't we get done—what are the things we chose to deprioritize and put in our backlog of work? The time between sprints is an opportunity for candid conversations among the team about how to improve for the next delivery cycle. How did our process work for us? Are we doing the work right? A discussion around these questions empowers the team to know they can get better at what they're trying to accomplish. They don't need a leader to hold them accountable to improve. Building in this process of candid reflection is part of teamship's contract of peer-to-peer accountability. It fits the pattern of team behavior all the way through the sprint: at every stand-up and Stress Test, team members are asked, *How can this project be better? How can we create more value? How can we do a better job for our customers?* To pivot to a better solution is always the best choice because it is the right choice for customers.

As for leaders, we have already noted, they do not micromanage agile teams, but ask strategic and reflective questions at review points, such as:

➤ What did we achieve in the last two weeks?

➤ Where did we struggle and why?

➤ What has changed in all key dimensions?

➤ Do we need to pivot?

➤ What will we achieve in the next two weeks?

➤ How can we measure the outcome?

The aim is always to improve behavior and processes, and ultimately customer outcomes, in the next sprint of work.

Teamship Practice: Foresight Five Minutes

As I explained in *Competing in the New World of Work*, our research shows that only 25 percent of Fortune 500 companies have some form of organic and regular team foresight practice—most of them lack a process to look for danger on the road ahead, or opportunities to elevate and go faster.

Foresight is the systematic ability to explore new break-through possibilities to avoid unsuspected risk and find unexpected growth. There is a really simple practice to help your organization constantly own the act of seeing around corners.

1. Reserve part of your monthly agenda for a Foresight Five Minutes. Every member of your team has been assigned to own and constantly research one vantage point of risk and opportunity. One will look at customer changes. Another will look at the world relative to technological changes. Another will look at macroeconomic policies or competition, or whatever the vantage point. Eventually you will even have AIs assigned such vantage points.
2. Then ask, "What risks and opportunities do we need to potentially move into analysis?"
3. You should go around and hear the answer verbally, or ideally you can put it into a shared document in advance.

At Lockheed Martin, prior to the COVID shutdown in the United States in 2020, somebody said, "I've been reading some blogs about some virus in China. It's a risk that we might want to move into assessment." They discussed it in a separate assessment meeting and moved it into a planning meeting. By February, they had moved out of their offices and gone fully virtual. Crowdsourcing foresight is a great opportunity to get ahead of problems before they land.

Teamship Practice: Decision Governance

Bold and inclusive team decision-making at the speed of today's volatile environment demands a standard process. Peer-to-peer collaboration does not mean someone does not have to make a final decision—or that everything has to run by consensus. In fact we are clear we do not believe in consensus but instead bold decision-making from broad and diverse opinions. It then demands clarity about who will make the final decision. World-class teams like Amazon use frameworks like DACI (Driver, Approver, Contributor, Informed) to ensure everyone is clear about roles and decision-making responsibilities and document who plays which role in a shared document. This should be a part of your agile team discussion.

Here's how it works.

➤ **Driver:** The person responsible for making sure everyone in the process has the information they need at the right time to participate and that actions and next steps are completed on time.

➤ **Approver:** This is the designated final decision maker.

➤ **Contributors:** Key team members and stakeholders who will participate in the agile process and help to shape the final decision made by the Approver through stand-up, CPS, and Stress Testing participation.

➤ **Informed:** People who will be affected by the final decision who need to be aware of the process and the next steps following its outcome and are best to involve in Stress Testing as they will share risks and innovation closest to the work itself.

As a Co-elevating team where the load of leadership is shared, the Approver role is not necessarily played by the leader. Instead, the Approver may be the executive sponsoring the project in play or running the division at the center of a transformation program or innovation initiative.

ENGINEERING THE FUTURE OF WORK

Few leaders really geek out on engineering their team behaviors and cultures of their companies. But those who do are typically engineers, like Arvind Krishna at IBM, who have turned their attention to not only the meticulous engineering of their products but also their processes and ways of working. These are the rare 15 percent. And every time, it reaps huge rewards for them, whether that's Drew Houston, who was a computer scientist, or Patti Poppe, an industrial engineer. What Krishna's work at IBM shows is that agile is no longer a methodology for IT teams; it's the operating system all teams need to be radically adaptable in today's volatile world.

CHAPTER 8

SHIFTING FROM A CULTURE OF SCARCE PRAISE TO PEER CELEBRATION AND RECOGNITION

Red Flag Rule:
We celebrate each other.

I t is hard to imagine starting a new job at a time with less cause for celebration than Carol Clements's first day. When she joined JetBlue as chief digital and technology officer, in the middle of the COVID pandemic, they had a fleet of seventy jets grounded in the desert. Nevertheless, the affordable-fares airline had ambitious plans to grow its 5 percent share of the US market. Of all the things that could have caught Clements's attention, there was a staff engagement survey waiting in her inbox that flagged low team morale, fatigue, and a lack of employee recognition as issues voiced by the organization's IT professionals—issues that many organizations face but that were certainly amplified in a COVID environment. Her team felt like they were too behind the scenes, with the wider company not always understanding or seeing their contributions, "a black box," as Clements describes it. Doing nothing wasn't an option. Like many technology leaders at the beginning of the pandemic, Clements and her team were faced with pressure to deliver technology that could help the company survive the effects of the pandemic, and to do so more quickly than ever before. Everyone in the world was fatigued, frustrated, and fearful. But Clements's experience both within travel at Southwest Airlines and outside the industry as CTO of Pizza Hut had taught her that she needed to first fill her team's tank before launching the technology transformation required to propel JetBlue through the pandemic and come out the other side positioned for success. She also knew it was not just about a show of rally and support from her at the top. It had to be richer, deeper, and more visible and on the front line where people were working, including the company as a whole. Clements says, "It's not uncommon in IT, but our team wasn't sure how they were contributing to the overall bigger picture of the company or broader initiatives. Ironically, that was great news because it's a pretty easy story to tell." Just as a leader might create a new social contract around a team giving each other feedback, Clements knew she needed to create a group effort around awakening the broader team to the hard and exceptional work that was taking place. Clements brought it up with JetBlue's executive team, and then made a person-to-person appeal to her new partners from outside the department to understand and articulate to her key staff, "This is how you're helping us deliver JetBlue's big-picture strategic priorities and we are so grateful." It made a huge difference because the team started to feel that their work mattered, not just for their colleagues, but for customers too. "Hey, I'm not just doing what my boss wants me to do and keeping her happy, this really matters to every one of our twenty-five thousand crew members and every single customer who flies JetBlue. People are recognizing what we are doing!" The movement was swift and the fuel in the tank could not have come at a more important time. Who knew that what was thought to be a few-month slowdown would turn into a multiyear global saga along with a talent crisis for her people's precise skill sets.

From there, Clements could start to build a more intimate culture of celebration and recognition among her IT group that she knew was the core to successful operations under great demand and stress. It started with the hiring process. When she is onboarding, she asks two questions and shares them broadly with the person's new team:

➤ What motivates you?
➤ How do you like to be recognized?

"I want the whole team to know what gets their peers out of bed every day and what makes them excited about their job," she says. "What's a meaningful way for them to uniquely feel like they are doing a good job and feel like they are valued? That usually spurs a pretty good conversation among the team with the new candidate from the start. From there, I ask the team to remember to be attuned to tailoring recognition for each other." This isn't about passing a formal note to HR. Clements has committed the answers to memory for her extended leadership team and she models this and calls it out as coaching for others to follow. For some team members, it's the big shout-out and moment of celebration with peers when JetBlue's senior leaders are in the room that matters and fuels teamship. For others, a celebration should be a more muted affair. "I've got one leader in particular who's very, very humble, and she never wants the attention," says Clements. "She loves to get her team in the spotlight. But leaders need to understand that their personal recognition can give their team a boost too. So, every once in a while, I'm going to push her out of her comfort zone because I want her to get the credit she deserves in front of people too." Looking back, the data at JetBlue suggests that Clements's approach to celebration and recognition has made a significant impact on the retention of tech talent in the business. Voluntary separation has decreased by 40 percent versus 2021 and was now at a five-year low. Regrettable loss was reduced by 65 percent over the same period and was also at a five-year low. Staff surveys showed that recognition shifted from being a significant detractor of engagement to being a promoter of it. "We are moving in the right direction," says Clements. "There is still work to do—I'm very proud but I'm not sure I'll ever be fully satisfied! There are always opportunities to do an even better job supporting our incredible IT organization."

APPLAUDING MARATHON RUNNERS
THROUGHOUT THE RACE

Our research shows that teams don't celebrate enough. Leaders are tough on themselves, particularly entrepreneurs (I know I always have been), and, as a result, they can be equally tough on others (I know I always have been). They are constantly pushing their teams to stretch for what's next. Our research shows that 79 percent of the people leaving organizations cite a lack of recognition as the primary reason for deciding to exit and pursue their careers elsewhere. Forty percent of employees report never getting recognition on the job. Even 50 percent of managers admit they do not recognize outstanding performance as they should. Let's think of work like a marathon race we're all running together. Along that marathon, how many people are dotting the streets, clapping, and encouraging and bringing energy to those runners to go faster? There's a celebration for people crossing the finish line at the end, but how many people would have gotten that far without the encouragement and celebration along the way?

A common question from leaders is, "Should I celebrate someone who is not doing that well?" The answer is yes. If someone struggles and you don't celebrate them, you keep pushing them down. Their energy is going to get lower and lower, and you'll get less and less out of them. High expectations and celebrations aren't mutually exclusive. You can set clear and appropriately high expectations for people even if they're not achieving them along the way. But the shift that's needed is that the whole team celebrates and lifts someone who is struggling. The team celebrates the things that they are achieving and celebrates them for things that you want them to achieve. Hard-driving leaders sometimes think that it's not the case. Remember, marathon runners need applause all the way. It's especially important for young team members who need to know that they're growing in the right direction, even though they're learning.

TEAMSHIP PRACTICES

After completing the diagnostic and establishing the Red Flag Rule, five teamship practices and our diagnostic exercise support the shift from a culture of scarce praise to peer-to-peer celebration and recognition. The teamship practices are a blend of impromptu action, habitual behavior in every meeting, and a cycle of weekly and monthly recognition that build a cadence of celebratory practice into teamship:

1. **Seeding Recognition:** An impromptu but intentional practice to celebrate individuals by dropping praise you know will get back to them.
2. **Gratitude Circle:** A positive reflective practice at the end of every meeting.
3. **Exploits of the Week:** A weekly celebration of achievements by the team.
4. **Peer Celebration:** A monthly round-robin peer-to-peer appreciation exercise.
5. **Formal Celebration:** More traditional leader-led celebration of the team and individual achievement every month.

The Celebration Diagnostic

STEP ONE: *Team Discussion About Peer Celebration and Recognition*

Are you a team that is constantly celebrating the wins of each other, lifting each other up? Lots of teams don't celebrate enough, particularly ones led by people who are tough on themselves. Those teams tend to focus on things that aren't done versus what is done. But if you want to find examples of teams that are great at recognition, the best sales organizations do this beautifully, always celebrating their wins.

STEP TWO: *Diagnostic Question*

All team members give a score of 1 to 5 for the following question (1: Strongly disagree, 2: Disagree, 3: Neutral, 4: Agree, 5: Strongly agree):

➤ All team members encourage and celebrate one another's success.

The diagnostic must be administered by a team member who is seen as agnostic and trusted, as the scoring is private and will not be attributed to individuals. Use an online survey tool or the Diagnostic Assessment on my website.

Red Flag Rule and Red Flag Replays

The Red Flag Rule for team behavior for celebration and recognition is: "We celebrate each other." Calling for a Red Flag Replay on this particular shift within a month of practicing the below teamship practices and then regularly thereafter is an opportunity to hold space to talk about where things may have gone off the rails, to check that our new behavioral commitments are being observed and teamship practices are being implemented.

Teamship Practice: Seeding Recognition

As a leader, go around and drop praise that you know will get back to the individual through the people meaningful to that person: their teammates, their boss, their associates, and perhaps even their parents. I had an extraordinary young man at Ferrazzi Greenlight named Frank Congiu. I had done a lot to make sure Frank knew he was valued, but at dinner one evening I heard of his father's weak health and some strained relationships within the family. I got the phone number for his dad and while he didn't answer, I left a message: "Mr. Congiu, I'm Keith Ferrazzi. Your son works for me. He doesn't know I'm calling but I wanted to congratulate you. The son you raised is truly exceptional. He outworks and outperforms individuals with years more experience. Whatever you did, it worked, and I just wanted to say thank you from the bottom of my heart." Frank found out about this when his father told him with tears how proud he was of his son. These were not words that Frank had heard before. And years later, when his dad passed, Frank found out he had saved that message and would listen to it often.

Teamship Practice: Gratitude Circle

The Gratitude Circle is a practice for use at the end of every meeting to focus on the positive and express gratitude for what's just occurred. Incorporating this practice is a way to end the meeting on a high note. Everyone goes around in turn and says what they are most grateful for from the meeting itself. Tell the group, "Okay, an hour ago you walked into this room and an hour later what are you most grateful for?" This is one where you don't have to lead, as the tone is fairly clear and not in need of vulnerability.

Teamship Practice: Exploits of the Week

One simple practice I learned of on a sales team's weekly call is to ask for news of "exploits of the week." These are the key wins, strategic moves, or examples of operational teamwork across functions that stand out that week. It's about highlighting individuals or specific teams for praise but also about reinforcing behaviors we want to see—like the cross-functional thinking and customer obsession that it takes to win in this competitive marketplace.

Teamship Practice: Peer Celebration

Peer Celebration is a round-robin share that we suggest teams do monthly, in which each team member takes turns sharing their appreciation for a peer or someone on a peer's team. The expression of appreciation should be specific—and it's an opportunity to reinforce positive behaviors from the team's new social contract.

To implement Peer Celebration:

Schedule time in the agenda. This allows everyone to prepare and think about this practice in advance, even ask members of their team for their ideas. Ideally, you would have at least 1–2 minutes per person for sharing and 2–3 minutes to set up the exercise. If you are short on time, instead of doing a round-robin in which everyone shares, be clear about the amount of time available and only choose a volunteer subset of participants to share.

Frame the exercise. Explain to participants that they will have the opportunity to share their gratitude for another team member. Tell participants that this is a chance to show how they appreciate the hard work that their colleagues put forth in service of their common goals. It is also an opportunity to forge deeper personal connections, so note that there is no reason to shy away from integrating the personal and professional in the expression of gratitude.

Invite silent reflection. Before beginning, invite the group to pause for a moment and consider silently what they are grateful for. Be explicit that they should ask themselves:

➤ For whom am I grateful?

➤ Why am I grateful for this person?

➤ How has this person positively impacted me and/or the team?

Setting this time aside first is important as it allows everyone to actively listen to the recognition others share instead of spending the time thinking about what they will say when it is their turn to speak.

Start sharing. Once you have given participants a moment to think about what they are grateful for, the group leader should share their gratitude first so they can model what is the appropriate level of depth and tone for the rest of the participants.

Below is a sample share that illustrates the kind of story a facilitator might offer to kick off the sharing:

I am grateful for Monica's help this past week rolling out the marketing initiative to go along with our new suite of cloud-based products. As you all know, I am a software engineer by training, and while I am knowledgeable about marketing the product, positioning and words really are not a core strength. Monica took two hours out of her busy day last week, and we did a deep dive into the marketing strategy her team had been developing. I was really impressed, and I left the conversation with actionable insights that we are going to integrate into our first rollout. I also found out that Monica and a few people from her group go running on Sunday nights, so I'll be able to join her in that as well. Thank you, Monica, I am extremely grateful for your partnership.

Here are a few tips to avoid platitudes:

➤ Use examples and short narratives to give your gratitude greater meaning and depth. Adding this degree of personalization also helps eliminate duplicate comments and keeps the session richer and more engaging.

➤ Offer details about how the person created a positive impact. This enriches the feedback and elevates it from appreciation to communications coaching that others can learn from and replicate.

➤ Minimize interruptions. It is critical to give individuals uninterrupted airtime while expressing gratitude; this is not the time for individuals to ask questions of each other. While it is okay to provide commentary, encourage your colleagues to keep their comments succinct, positive, and reserved for only after the individual in the spotlight has finished speaking.

➤ Acknowledge each other's growth. Encourage participants to consider sharing their gratitude for how their teammates are living their commitments and being accountable for results.

Teamship Practice: Formal Celebration

Scheduling formal leader-nominated celebrations of key teammates' efforts and wins is also really important. Doing this sets a standard every month for what good is and what should be celebrated and what others should aspire to do and achieve.

WE ALL NEED RECOGNITION

"I've done over 35,000 interviews in my career, and as soon as that camera shuts off, everyone always turns to me and inevitably, in their own way, asks this question: '*Was that okay?*'" Oprah Winfrey once said. "I heard it from President Bush. I heard it from President Obama. I've heard it from heroes and from housewives. I've heard it from victims and perpetrators of crimes. I even heard it from Beyoncé in all of her Beyoncé-ness." It's the story of how we all, however grand or humble, need validation. We all need celebration and recognition. The behavioral economist and my friend Dan Ariely once said that public recognition is more motivating than financial recognition. Let's make sure that team celebration and recognition are used abundantly.

CHAPTER 9

SHIFTING TO DIVERSITY, INCLUSION, AND BELONGING

Red Flag Rule:
We believe a diversity of people and voices achieves breakthrough performance.

I was invited to Geneva by the World Economic Forum in January 2023 to host two sessions with business leaders and senior politicians on diversity, equity, and inclusion. I took the opportunity to ask the assembled leaders, thinkers, and practitioners a simple question: *If you had a team to coach for six months to be the shining emblem of DEI, what would you do?* Much has been written and said about enterprise HR DEI practices that typically focus on driving better enterprise representation and fairness, and rightly so, but how we interact as diverse, equitable, and inclusive teams remains an undercurated and underexplored topic. The answers I heard from leaders in Geneva, and many discussions with deeply committed leaders since then, have led our research to see the importance of teams adopting the following set of new team behaviors and practices:

➤ **Inclusion.** The high-return practices in chapters 3 (candor), 6 (collaboration and co-creation), and 7 (agile) along with the chapter to come on professional development are a prescription for inclusion and opening collaboration to all individuals, ensuring that all voices have the highest likelihood of being heard and considered. Monica Pool Knox, two-time CHRO, tech advisor, and board member, points out "the opportunity for teams to seek out, recognize, leverage, and relish the unique experiences and perspectives of their teammates." She adds, "Recognizing the bright lines of our differences and leaning into it can spark innovative ideas, challenge conventional ways of thinking, and birth new approaches that improve processes, create new products, different ways to connect with and win the trust of customers."

➤ **Belonging.** At their core, dream teams invest in and build strong relational bonds, as chapter 4 has shown. Their commitment to serve, care, and share with each other—and in chapter 5 (resilience) to lift each other up when support is needed—builds a strong connection and belonging within the team.

➤ **Otherness.** Samantha, one senior HR leader I spoke to, was foremost among the executives to raise the topic of otherness. She said that she strives to help all of her teams understand that, at different times, we all know what it feels like to be "other." And, as another Fortune 100 leader said to me, we have to work hard to bridge otherness. Particularly in the age of global business and global clients, we must all strive to see the world through other people's eyes and other cultural perspectives if we want our organizations to succeed.

➤ **Privilege and Obstacles.** As Khalil Smith, vice president of inclusion, diversity, and engagement at Akamai Technologies, told me, "Privilege is not unique to a particular demographic, and neither are obstacles unique to a particular demographic—and these two things are not mutually exclusive." Discussing privilege and overcoming obstacles is one of the most sensitive but productive conversations teams can have.

INCLUSION LEADS TO A BILLION-DOLLAR INNOVATION

The simple truth is that greater inclusion leads to greater outputs—it's an echo of the shift to broader, more inclusive co-creation we discussed in chapter 6. Pool Knox gives the example of her experience at Frito-Lay as part of the organization's Hispanics for Excellence Employee Resource Group (an underrepresented demographic at the company). She describes how the group came up with the idea for a billion-dollar brand:

> I remember when we began talking about the opportunity to create a flavored chip that appealed to the palate of the Latin American consumer (being in Texas, employees who worked at the company knew the spices that appealed to the palate of those whose family roots stemmed from south of the border were quite different). After Frito-Lay's food scientists experimented with flavors common to Central and South America, the Jalapeno chip flavor was born. It was a hit.

Shifting to diversity, inclusion, and belonging is embracing all the talent in your organization, expanding the opportunity for all perspectives to be heard, and igniting the possibility of greater innovation.

Yet if we need to be reminded of the cost of inaction or failing to embrace the broadest talent available to us, Pool Knox has another career lesson we can learn from. She tells of an experience in one organization where a sales team went to pitch to potential customers. The pitch was eloquent and the customer thanked them for their time and the sales team returned to the office feeling cautiously optimistic. Yet the customer got back in touch quickly to say they had decided to buy from a competitor. It was clear the sales team had not won the customer's trust and it had happened early in the process. Pool Knox explains that the sales team of four white, middle-aged straight men had made little connection with the four-woman customer team made up of two white women, one Asian woman, and one African American woman. She says:

> The customer team not only felt the sales team communicated in a way that did not resonate with them, but also felt there was not a shared sense of values around the importance of diverse perspectives, approaches and experiences. The company lost the business because they didn't adequately do their homework, read the room and understand how they were communicating their values. The irony is that my company in fact did not have a female sales leader to send with the team. If we had, we would have recognized the sales team we were sending to meet with this customer team was not optimal. The customer was in many ways spot-on.

One of the sessions I facilitated in Geneva was about how we as leaders might change the slope of the curve on the gender pay gap with a set of clear springs over the next seven years. If we don't take action, at the current rate of progress, we'll achieve parity in 151 years. That's not a typo. One hundred and fifty-one years. Nine out of ten leaders of the world's biggest companies say that diversity is more important than ever before. But we are still at the beginning of our journey. Only 12 percent of Fortune 100 CEOs are women, and 14 percent are ethnically diverse. Not accepting the status quo is the first high-return practice.

Why do we need diversity? Because it gives us better answers. We need our teams to align with the values and sentiments and reflect the world we are in—and selling to. Later in the chapter there is a teamship practice that addresses this point directly about hiring talent that was suggested by Enrique Lores, the CEO of HP, who makes the same point: we need teams to resonate with the world we live in. It's a business-critical issue.

TEAMSHIP PRACTICES

Three teamship practices support the shift to diversity, inclusion, and belonging:

1. **Otherness:** A storytelling team exercise where team members share examples of when they felt "other."

2. **Privilege and Obstacles:** The partner teamship practice to Otherness, a round-robin exercise about how the invisible hand of privilege has opened career doors to team members and what obstacles they have faced in their career path.

3. **Hold for the Right Slate:** This is a simple practice for ensuring that your team has the highest-caliber candidates and is also diverse.

In this shift, our research institute still has much work to do. Our diagnostic data is still not statistically significant, and data-gathering is still underway.

Red Flag Rule and Red Flag Replays

The simple teamship social contract for diversity, inclusion, and belonging is, "We believe a diversity of people and voices achieves breakthrough performance." Calling for a Red Flag Replay on this particular shift within a month of practicing the below teamship practices and then regularly thereafter is an opportunity to hold space to talk about where things may have gone off the rails, to check that our new behavioral commitments are being observed and teamship practices are being implemented.

Teamship Practice: Otherness

Enrique Lores, the CEO of HP (previously Hewlett-Packard), speaks eloquently about how diversity in his team is the best way to ensure they can run a successful business with customers worldwide. But highlighting team members' differences, their *otherness*, is also a constructive way of bringing different perspectives to the table that unlock business decisions, he says. "Because of my accent and where I went to school, I'm not the typical Fortune 50 CEO that has gone to one of the Ivy League schools and speaks perfect English," says Lores. "By acknowledging that—and I do that whenever I think it is necessary—it's a way to make sure that everybody feels encouraged to talk more candidly about when they feel 'other.' I think it's also very important for all the senior team to do the same with their teams. They need to bring the vulnerability of their own lives into the conversation and the consequences of the experiences [they] have had. When we feel like outsiders, we are less likely to speak our minds. In addition to helping the team know that I too feel like an outsider at times, which helps us bridge our universal otherness, I also recognize that speaking up to power is something people need real-time coaching around. I will say, *'This is what I think, but please, many of you who feel differently, I really do appreciate your views so I can have better data for my conclusions.'* It's a way of generating better ideas and better views and richer conversations."

The otherness idea was operationalized at HP with an exercise aimed at finding sameness, similar to the exercises we describe in team bonding, where the senior team was broken into pairs to discuss their life stories, the triumphs and tragedies in their lives. "By doing that in very small groups, people were more willing to really open themselves and to share both things that had really brought joy to their lives, but also their tragedies and how these things have been impacting their learnings or their careers or their choices," says Lores. "When you know and you understand someone more deeply the inevitable conclusion that people come away from is universal empathy, that in our struggles and joys we are more alike than different. We are fundamentally human first."

The power of otherness is that it recognizes that the workplace is a microcosm of society. We have different passions, ideas, and beliefs, as well as backgrounds. We need to celebrate and appreciate our differences but approach them sensitively and with respect rather than as grounds for conflict. This teamship practice is to share in a round-robin session with the team one moment when you have felt "other." The first person to share in the round-robin should be one who is willing to share vulnerably. Personally, I have felt other when I was younger at Yale, ashamed of my blue-collar unemployed family upbringing, in my freshman orientation. I felt other when, in my first job after Yale, I would hear my boss tell gay jokes or offhanded derogatory remarks about an effeminate coworker.

There is no invitation for cross talk in this share, just listening and appreciating how others have felt when they felt "other." The challenge of teamship is to recognize and appreciate all those who are different and who have different perspectives on the world—and to be inclusive of those perspectives, political or otherwise.

Teamship Practice: Privilege and Obstacles

I've encountered a lot of fear and uncertainty about how to start—whether to even try to start—team discussions about privilege. Conversations with Khalil Smith at Akamai Technologies helped to frame an entry point, and I think it's worth quoting him in full:

> Privilege is not unique to a particular demographic, and obstacles are not unique to a particular demographic— and these two things are not mutually exclusive. Your privilege doesn't mean you didn't work hard as hell. The

fact that you worked hard as hell doesn't mean you didn't have a leg up on somebody else. Sometimes when we hear *privilege*, we think everything has been handed to someone. You need to get that out of the way up front. If you grew up with a lot of money, that's privileged, it doesn't mean your father wasn't an asshole, it doesn't mean that your mother loved you. It doesn't mean that you didn't work hard when you got your MBA. I'm just saying it's easier to have money than to not, it's easier to be attractive than to be ugly. That's what we're getting at. At that point, maybe people will say, "*Oh yeah, you're right*. I did have some of these things. But that doesn't mean I didn't work hard. And I have had some obstacles. But that doesn't mean that things weren't handed to me."

Having a round-robin conversation with the team about privilege and obstacles is a partner practice to Otherness. Until the team has developed a foundation of trust through the practices of this book, it may be helpful to facilitate this conversation through a coach. As anyone who has read my first book, *Never Eat Alone*, knows, I grew up in a poor household with working-class parents and worked hard for everything I have. But look at my story another way. My father was deeply committed to me getting a great education and instilled in me a commitment to my studies and a drive toward high levels of achievement. I'm a white, twice Ivy League–educated man who has worked in the C-suite of Fortune 500 companies. If that doesn't scream privilege, I don't know what does. I have not faced sexism or racism (other than through the eyes and experiences of my adopted children). I hid my being gay amid frequent homophobic comments in the workplace by senior people and mentors. Would I be in the fortunate position to have had the success I did at an early age that allowed me to write this book if I had come out openly? Perhaps not. That's the honesty of a Privilege and Obstacles practice. In that round-robin conversation—as I suggest, facilitated if necessary, until the team has developed the necessary trust and psychological safety—everyone takes turns to briefly acknowledge where the invisible hand of privilege has opened career doors to them and what obstacles they have faced in their career path. It's not about victims or villains. It's about understanding who we all are and the hidden advantages and obstacles that we've experienced along the way.

Teamship Practice: Hold for the Right Slate

Before he was appointed HP CEO, Lores ran a project to diversify the company's board, and he translated that same success into his executive team. I asked him what his key takeaway from the experience was. "If your slate of candidates for a senior role isn't diverse enough, *wait until it is*," he said. "Candidates from a diverse range of backgrounds are there if you are diligent enough to seek them." That was so powerful in its simplicity. If in your first round of recruitment, you don't have a diverse slate of candidates, you need to try again. And again, until you do. The candidates are there. If candidates are not coming forward for your vacancy, there are deeper questions you need to ask about diversity, equity, and inclusion in your organization.

VALUES AND BELONGING

It may seem strange to discuss exclusions in a chapter with inclusion at its heart. But in conversation with Khalil Smith, the word *exclusion* took on a new meaning. "The best teams are exclusive around values, inclusive around demographics," Smith said. Can you work in a senior team at Apple without being passionate about design? Can you work at Nike without thinking anyone can take up a sport? Can you work at Philip Morris if you don't believe in personal choice? Some things are so connected to corporate values that they are necessary to succeed in a team in those organizations.

CHAPTER 10

SHIFTING TO A TEAM OF SEEKERS WHO ARE EACH OTHER'S COACHES

Red Flag Rule:
We coach each other.

What's the secret of a disrupter that can shake up an industry dominated by legacy brands like L'Oréal and Estée Lauder and then continue to sustain accelerated growth and innovation over twenty years? Look at the cosmetics company e.l.f. Beauty (Eyes, Lips, Face). You might first think that the secret is that back in 2004 it broke the rules by betting that people would buy lipstick and skin care online for one dollar when all the conventional wisdom said these were intimate choices about color, texture, and style that would always be made in person, in store. But fast-forward twenty years when all the competition is also battling it out online and you will find e.l.f. still disrupting and defying the industry wisdom by bringing high-quality products to market from concept to online launch in as few as thirteen weeks, while the average industry new product cycle can take 2–3 years depending on the company. The answer is not some product or manufacturing process secret. Don't be dazzled by e.l.f.'s many first-mover achievements, though they do provide true differentiation. You would be missing the real secret sauce. The team behaviors embedded in e.l.f. act as the farm from which such achievements repeatedly grow. According to e.l.f.'s executive team, "There is no place like e.l.f." and they take very seriously what it means to be ambassadors of e.l.f.-like team culture. In the financial year ending March 2023, net sales rose 48 percent, to $578.8 million. This is a business that has seen an 84-fold increase in shareholder value in a decade to $11 billion. By reputation, e.l.f. is great at leveraging customer feedback—more than 130,000 product reviews on its website (great, good, and not so good, transparency is all)—and soaking up data from its social media channels and millions-strong community to predict changing trends and tastes. But again, that's just what we see from the outside. When sitting down with Chairman and CEO Tarang Amin and his executive team, I learned the key is that they are focused relentlessly on creating a high-impact team and investing in teamship. It's not just that all full-time employees are on a single bonus plan tied to a financial earnings target (adjusted EBITDA) and receive an equity award in e.l.f. stock, which is a big deal. It's constant performance development. It's about creating an ever-present peer-to-peer coaching culture within and among the teams.

CO-ELEVATION COACHING IN ACTION

Mandy Fields, e.l.f. Beauty's CFO, describes how Kory Marchisotto, the CMO, coached her to become a better storyteller. "I have gotten feedback that I just go directly to an answer when I get questions from investors and analysts," says Fields. "Kory's feedback was 'Hey, back up a little bit, take them through how you got there, and then answer the question.' And so I have tried to incorporate that in what I do." In turn, Fields has also coached Marchisotto. "Kory is a superstar and one of the best marketers I have ever met. And I said to her, if she aspires to be more than CMO, let me help you with some more nuanced financial elevation and brought her into the earnings process and investor conferences so that she really gets under the hood of what's happening financially and can ask even more thin-sliced questions." It's Co-elevation—the commitment to the mission and commitment to care about each other enough not to let each other fail—in practice.

This new approach to feedback and its link to personal development and achievement and business outcomes is a fundamentally different social contract than most of us have experienced elsewhere. It all starts with a very aspirational set of promises for every associate that we all actively need to fulfill for each other. As Marchisotto explains:

At e.l.f., we are invited to find and unleash our absolute best selves with the everyday support of those around us. You are invited into a culture that says, "I'm not trying to mold you or shape you. I'm trying to figure out, what does peak-state look like for you; what are your super-powers, and how do I help you unleash them so that you can be increasingly the best version of yourself?" That already changes people's mindsets. It changes their purpose for and approach to receiving and giving feedback. Feedback is not chipping away at you, it does not feel like rocks being handed to you, weighing you down with each piece of feedback. In fact, it is the helium that raises all balloons higher. You are operating in a zone where you really believe that everybody around you wants you to be the best you.

Whether you're an intern or a new VP, all new employees are taught during their onboarding at e.l.f. that growth and learning come from embracing candor and healthy challenge in a respectful way from your peers. You learn quickly both to assume that everyone has good intentions and to be attentive to how you can support and truly care about everyone's success—both are required and are the keynotes of coaching Co-elevation. And if your feathers get ruffled? If ever you are questioning the presence of that care and positive intent, it's expected that you will voice your concerns clearly and remain open to the fact that you may be mistaken once you hear the explanation. That means everyone has a responsibility to give each other feedback and to tell each other when they are not being as effective as they could be, even if it means respectfully pointing out the opportunities for growth of someone senior. At e.l.f. constant feedback is expected and welcomed 360 degrees around. If you hear a member of the leadership team saying something you don't think is right, you speak up. But what new recruits don't get at e.l.f. is traditional episodic quarterly or annual reviews. The feedback dialogue is not a top-down monologue from the manager dressed up as a discussion. Instead, it's happening every day, it's ongoing, and it's coming from all directions and all quarters that you interact with in your day-to-day work, independent of the organizational hierarchy. And it is coached and reinforced in every team by leaders and teammates who prize this cultural norm.

Kerry Preston, e.l.f. Beauty's vice president of people development, explains that in addition to the everyday feedback and coaching, twice a year teams will come together to proactively and purposefully offer each other open feedback (see the high-return practice Open 360). They will give each other specific examples of what they admire most about each other, what they think limits each other's effectiveness, and how they can support each other in the future. In one session, a senior e.l.f. exec was called out for canceling four out of five one-on-one meetings with someone on their team. "When you cancel meetings like that, it's not so much a question of jeopardizing our performance but it's about respect," they were told. "Let's talk about how we can perhaps approach time management differently." In another team session, a teammate was encouraged by peers to speak up more in meetings. Another teammate's solution? "We'll get you to speak first, okay?"

At e.l.f., the culmination of the culture comes to fruition with employees' invitation to the major product innovation meeting, what Amin describes as "the hottest ticket in town." Every employee has an open invite to shape the future of the product roadmap in their sight of responsibility. It's a time for strong debate and no holds barred. It's exciting and fast and only possible after years of practice in a culture that holds nothing back. Everyone knows they need to make their point and be prepared to develop their argument; to give candid feedback but do so respectfully. They know the best argument and the best idea will win. That's how e.l.f. is elevating individual development through constant peer-to-peer feedback and in turn elevating its business.

THE FEEDBACK FRAMEWORK

Amin's product innovation meeting is a great example of the importance of candid feedback on ideas as discussed in chapter 3. Everyone talks about feedback as if it's one thing. But we need to think about it in a new way. There are different types of feedback and those differences matter. Peers need to challenge each other and give feedback about:

1. **Ideas.** This is about candid feedback on ideas and the ability to wrestle ideas to the boldest and most inclusive

solutions. Peers need to use high-return practices to be more courageous while they co-create and collaborate (chapter 6).

2. **Performance.** Peers need to hold each other accountable for delivery, as we discussed in chapters 3 (candor) and 7 (agile). The Stress Testing teamship practice, in which someone represents what they believe they have achieved and the group challenges if they see otherwise, is the common element in performance feedback.

3. **Competencies.** This is the new social contract for this chapter. Peers need to challenge each other to update and upgrade their skills and knowledge to be of the highest caliber in their field, one who embraces new and emerging technologies and ways of working. This is precisely what the peer-to-peer coaching by Mandy Fields, the CFO, and Kory Marchisotto, the CMO, at e.l.f. illustrates.

4. **Style.** Peers need to challenge each other on their working styles, which include communication and ways of motivating and creating followership. Procrastination and poor time management are basic style problems, so the team might give feedback to move to more pro-activity. Another example is to have less of a victim mindset of blaming others or adopt a growth mindset like an entrepreneur instead of only seeing blockers to progress.

Some companies are decent at challenging and giving feedback on business ideas but have little to no permission to comment on each other's performance, skills, competencies, or style. As we saw in chapter 3, candor in most firms ranks only 2.4 on a 5-point scale. In most companies, rarely have they activated any degree of peer-to-peer coaching. Our research shows that 71 percent of team members are not committed to elevating their coworkers by offering feedback on their work. Imagine the burden lifted off the average manager when this contract is adopted; you will recall from chapter 2 that when peer-to-peer teamship was activated by Sergey Young, he recovered 30 percent of his time for more strategic thinking and longer-term projects.

We give feedback to our peers as a data point that shows our commitment to each other's success on the path to winning together. It's also a critical part of the new social contract of teamship because the old contract, where a manager is the sole source of feedback, is increasingly impractical. For decades now with the flattening of organizational structures, it has been more and more difficult for managers to be effective coaches. Managers may not even have adequate visibility into the day-to-day work of individuals or their teams. Who does have that visibility? The team members who are working together, independent of org charts. It's the people working alongside us every day who see our efforts, challenges, and successes. They're in a prime position to offer relevant, timely feedback—and we need to leverage this abundant yet virtually untapped resource and insight.

There is also a false belief among people who reach the leader ranks that they need less development than they did during earlier stages of their careers—and indeed, in most organizations the further up the organizational ladder people progress, the less feedback they are apt to receive. But we leaders need coaching too, particularly around team behaviors. "Too often, the assumption in business is that everyone who has reached seniority is great at giving and receiving feedback. Most people aren't," says Amin. "So, we do sessions as a senior team and we role-model peer-to-peer feedback." Particularly in today's ever-changing business environment, individuals at every level must continually improve and grow. We cannot possibly think we are equipped for what is happening around the corner. We *must* get 30–50 percent better every year to keep up with the pace of change. And this extreme number is important because anything short of such a radical improvement would leave us comfortable with incremental change and not actively seeking the discomfort that may be associated with this extreme feedback culture.

The highest-performing teams we've worked with have had social contracts allowing members to transparently give one another feedback on performance, skills and competencies, and work style in service of growth. But 61 percent of team members in our dataset said that they do not see their peers as having the humility to see their own personal development or growth needs and seek improvement. Presumably, people fail to prioritize their own development because they are overwhelmed by heavy workloads and believe they lack the time. That belief creates a catch-22: without team-specific coaching and development, the work is indeed harder than it needs to be, and collaboration is less effective—so workloads become even heavier, making people feel even more overwhelmed and less able to pursue development and growth.

TEAMSHIP PRACTICES

After completing the diagnostic and establishing the Red Flag Rule, three simple teamship practices support the shift to become a team of peer-to-peer coaches and take the burden of feedback from overstretched leaders.

1. **Open 360:** A quarterly practice that reframes the traditional leader-to-direct-report appraisal meeting as a peer-to-peer team exercise.
2. **Dial Up/Dial Down:** Often follows on from the Open 360 but only takes a few minutes. It's a behavior-change commitment by each member of the team to their peers.
3. **5/5/5 Learning Roadmap:** Five minutes of sharing, five minutes of questions, five of advice. It's an accountability practice that ensures team members keep on track with their learning commitments.

The Development Diagnostic

STEP ONE: *Team Discussion About Co-Development*
This shift is toward co-development and an approach that transforms feedback from a one-way directive into a dynamic,

mutual growth process—*we become a team of seekers, committed to the mission and the elevation of each other.* In co-development, feedback isn't just a managerial task; it shifts to become a collective responsibility of us all. Every team member plays a part in elevating the group, sharing insights and skills to help each other thrive. We are each other's coaches and we would not dare to hold back. World-class teams typically score 4.4 out of 5 in our diagnostic. From my own experience, I've seen the transformative power of this approach firsthand. In my teams, I emphasize the importance of open, candid peer feedback. It's not just about doing our jobs; it's about helping each other grow and excel. But it's rare. Most teams score below 2.5 in our diagnostic.

Marchisotto describes a great example of the new social contract for development in action with one of the highest-performing members of the team: someone she describes as "a true visionary, a creative genius." But she explains: "It's hard to be a visionary because you can see things that other people can't see. And it can be a great frustration to get the work to the levels of quality that you can see in your brain if it's not even close yet." The creative's style of giving feedback was demotivating people and the work was further from achieving the original vision. There was frustration all around. In a team session, the creative was given feedback from their peers about their feedback style. In front of the team, the creative made a commitment to be more empathic in the future. "That particular individual said in front of all of their peers who have given that feedback, that they had heard them, that it's right, that they'll work on it, and they'll make a commitment to empathy," says Marchisotto. "It's extraordinary for someone to be that vulnerable in a room of seventeen people and make that kind of commitment. But the motivation was clear: the team was not at peak state and that needed to change."

Using the two questions of our Diagnostic Framework as cues is a great way to initiate a team discussion about the new social contract we want to follow in order to achieve a shift toward peer-to-peer co-development.

STEP TWO: *Diagnostic Questions*
All team members give a score of 1 to 5 for the following questions (1: Strongly disagree, 2: Disagree, 3: Neutral, 4: Agree, 5: Strongly agree):

➤ Are we a team of seekers? All team members are aware of and open about their areas of growth and are actively pursuing corrective development.

➤ Are we each other's coaches? All team members are personally invested in one another's development and are proactively providing peer-to-peer coaching on their teammates' performance and hard and soft skills and competencies.

The diagnostic must be administered by a team member who is seen as agnostic and trusted, as the scoring is private and will not be attributed to individuals. Use an online survey tool or the Diagnostic Assessment on my website.

Red Flag Rule and Red Flag Replays

The simple teamship social contract for development is "We coach each other." Calling for a Red Flag Replay on this particular shift within a month of practicing the below teamship practices and then regularly thereafter is an opportunity to hold space to talk about where things may have gone off the rails, to check that our new behavioral commitments are being observed and teamship practices are being implemented.

Teamship Practice: Open 360

We're all familiar with traditional 360 reviews: performance evaluations that solicit feedback from all directions, typically anonymously and in writing. An Open 360 is a round-robin format for giving and receiving individual feedback in a team setting. Every participant shares one thing they appreciate/admire/respect about each teammate and one thing they suggest the other person could do differently to elevate their performance and success further. This practice requires teammates to overcome conflict avoidance and engage in courageous candor in service of each other's greatness. For Open 360 to be effective, the team must have a basis of trust and commitment to one another's professional success and personal growth. If there is a lack of trust there will not be enough psychological safety for teammates to give each other the most impactful feedback, which sometimes may be hard to hear. It does not serve the person who is denied information that would make the biggest difference to their success.

It is for this reason that we wait to introduce Open 360 until the team has agreed upon the social contract and worked together on developing the relationship strength and empathy among them, as discussed in chapter 4. Once there is a basis of agreement and relatedness, team members can support each other by providing caring and candid feedback—an act of generosity—and holding themselves and each other accountable to act on it. To hold an Open 360:

1. **Introduce the idea.** For example, "This exercise is designed to get individual feedback from people while instilling greater candor and intimacy within our team. We'll all have a chance to give and receive feedback; to do that we'll need to keep comments to a minute or less."

2. **Set expectations.** "Let's avoid cross talk—you will be able to respond to all feedback at the end. When you receive your feedback, acknowledge that you heard it (say 'thank you') and resist the temptation to be defensive. Accept that any one person's perception is valid—it's just one data point and it's up to you to decide whether or not you want to adjust your behavior based on the perceptions of your teammates." Back in chapter 3 we talked about the historical reality that all feedback, whether from teachers, parents, or leaders, used to come with the requirement to do something about it. In this case, it does not. Peer-to-peer feedback is just data, it's not a directive. So, it need not be as full of expectation and defensiveness.

3. **Explain how it will work.**
   It's often best if the leader is the first to receive feedback.

On the first go-around, each team member will complete the sentence to the person receiving the feedback: "One thing I most appreciate/admire/respect about you is _____."

On the second go-around, each team member will complete the sentence "Because I care about you and your success, I might suggest _____." The presumption here is that not only do we care about this person's success, but their success is important to the team's success, which makes it important that the most impactful feedback is shared.

Open 360s can be done regularly, so refer feedback to performance over the last quarter or prior six months.

4. **Make these points about giving feedback.**

Comments should be additive, not duplicative, to save time. If someone has already made your intended comment, simply state, "I want to echo what [insert person's name] said."

In the second round of critical feedback, give the clearest, most tactical suggestions on how they can improve and elevate their performance.

Before sharing, ask yourself if the comments serve the other person and the team. The feedback should be about helping each other elevate our performance and improve as a team.

Feedback is a gift; you can't accelerate your performance, or career, without it.

Here's how it might play out.

"David, what I most admire about you is your work ethic and your commitment to your promises."

"Because I care about you and your success and your success is so important to our success, I might suggest that you appreciate others on this team who have different beliefs and boundaries around work and family and may not be as quick to respond to you on weekends, holidays, and evenings."

Keep in mind . . .

This can be a sensitive exercise among teams where the social contract is new, so your role as leader is to go first and really model welcoming the input.

If you sense apprehension about this exercise, remind participants that once the team gets more comfortable, the Open 360 exercise will be an effective tool for practicing giving feedback and closing what research shows is often a large gap between how we perceive ourselves and how others perceive us.

At the end of each round where each person has received both types of feedback, ask each person to say to the group what they are committing to, using the framework of "Yes, I will do this," and "I will consider this and want to seek more information about it."

After receiving feedback in an Open 360, also consider inviting other colleagues, like your direct reports, to be part of your learning journey by sharing a summary of the feedback you received and asking for their reaction and input. This is an effective way to model humility and invite your teammates to join you in your development.

The more broadly you share what you are working on and the more you invite others to hold you accountable, the more you strengthen the social contract while demonstrating your commitment to your personal learning journey.

Teamship Practice: Dial Up/Dial Down

Dial Up/Dial Down is a shorter exercise, and one more focused on self-reflection, which is one of the foundational elements of professional development. Simply put, it is the practice of examining that which you believe, based on all the information you have, is limiting your current level of performance and publicly committing to take action to do more (Dial Up) or do less (Dial Down) of a specific behavior or behaviors in order to grow personally and professionally. The Dial Up/Dial Down is about making a commitment to your personal growth and declaring to your team the actions you will take so they can hold you accountable.

INTRODUCING A DIAL UP/DIAL DOWN

1. Set aside time in your meeting for the activity. Budget five minutes to set up the exercise, five minutes for self-reflection, and one minute per person for sharing.
2. Define Dial Up and Dial Down. A Dial Up is a behavior you need to do more of to be more successful on behalf of the team. A Dial Down is a behavior you need to do less of or eliminate altogether.

3. Coach participants to find the right Dial Up and/or Dial Down. Consider the feedback you've received in the past, which of course can be through the Open 360 exercise. Also consider your goals and how you'll need to behave if you want to get to the next level.

   Consider your personal life. Think about feedback you have received from your spouse/significant other, family members, and/or friends. It is common that personal behaviors cascade into the professional, and vice versa.

4. Invite participants to commit to action by:

   ➤ Sharing their Dial Up/Dial Down with the team.
   ➤ Creating a visual reminder that helps them stay present to their commitment. For example, placing a Post-it near their desk or setting periodic reminders on their phone.
   ➤ Creating a habit or practice that will assist these changes, like setting digital reminders to assess your progress.

Dial Up/Dial Down is about being reflective and committing to your personal growth and declaring to your team the actions you will take so they can hold you accountable for going higher together.

Teamship Practice: 5/5/5 Learning Roadmap
In chapter 6 we talked about the importance of creating Relationship Action Plans (RAPs) to identify the key relationships

you need to engage your team to achieve your goals proactively. The same is true of your own development: you need a hard and soft skill Learning Roadmap that identifies not only the formal courses you can take but the informal learning you can engage in from people you admire to help you grow in the directions you need. As an individual and as a team you need to invest rich time and attention into building your Learning Roadmaps to ensure that your future developmental needs are covered. There is a general question and a specific one for each member of the team:

➤ What are your strengths and weaknesses and opportunities for growth—and where and from whom do you want to learn?
➤ What do you feel you need to learn to grow into your next position—and whom do you need to learn it from?

What follows next, the peer-to-peer Stress Test of your plan, is the key. Let your learning peer group guide you. Research shows it is best to match purpose with urgency and accountability, so we coach teams to share their Learning Roadmaps in peer coaching groups with 5/5/5 formats. Here's how it works. At regular intervals, each team member gives a five-minute update on their roadmap and how far they have progressed with closing the gaps through formal and informal mechanisms. The team peppers them with questions for the next five minutes about that roadmap and their growth success. It's essential to keep asking questions and not jump to making directive suggestions, as the questions are powerful both for the team to learn and further understand, but for the person describing their learning journey to come to their own conclusions, which are more sustainable than those from others. The final five minutes is spent with the team giving double-barrel feedback. The senior leaders at e.l.f. each have a Learning Roadmap and are engaged in regular 5/5/5 coaching sessions with their peers to be accountable for progress. Stretch goals for development are great—having accountable momentum toward achieving them is even better.

CO-DEVELOPMENT'S PAYOFF

The payoff of co-development at e.l.f. is an amazing business. At e.l.f. you grow faster and further and stronger than anywhere else you might have been—in a fast-paced, fast-growing business environment that is explosive with energy. There is a simple lesson for leaders in e.l.f.'s story. By embracing a culture of co-development, where feedback is a tool for collective elevation and business breakthroughs, we're not just enhancing our own development; we're fostering a more collaborative, empowered, and successful work environment. In this new world of work, feedback isn't just about correction—it's about connection, growth, and elevating each other to be our best selves in work and in life. This is the essence of co-development, and it's how we can all achieve extraordinary things together as a team.

SHIFTING FROM SILOS TO ALIGNMENT

Red Flag Rule:
*We are aligned on the North Star and the
priorities and trade-offs to get there.*

B y now you have gone through nine shifts, but one of
the biggest promises of this transparent and inclusive
model of teamship too often eludes organizations. It is
the clear alignment to a North Star, and also clarity around
the many trade-offs and priorities various parts of the organization need to make to get there. Siloed organizations are
unaware of the challenges and needs of their peers so they
maximize for their piece of the pie. But teamship allows not
only visibility but rich engagement across these silos so the
goals of the enterprise are kept forefront and the trade-offs

can be made in real time and constantly along the way. The promise of aligned focus on achieving extraordinary enterprise outcomes and results becomes each team's goal, along with delivering their own parts. So far, for the sake of focused coaching, we have drawn attention to a team's execution of a particular Red Flag Rule and the practices they relied on. In each instance, we could have used any of these teams as an example for any other shift. Their presence in this book as an example of teamship means they leveraged all the shifts to achieve breakthrough performance. In this chapter, we'll introduce three new teams who have been aggregating across these shifts to outperform their markets, and we invite you to join them in the shift to teamship and the Co-elevation behaviors.

PEER-TO-PEER CANDOR, ACCOUNTABILITY, AND COLLABORATION AT P&G

A vision of forty quarters of growth. "It had never been done before in the fabric and home care business," says Sundar Raman, chief executive officer of Procter & Gamble's largest business sector. "Each of us had to constantly look both short- and long-term toward the same ultimate and collective end. And it was a game changer. It brought about a deep emotional commitment. It was palpable in the room whenever we got together. We had such clear alignment under only one North Star." The stark clarity and such alignment flow from the constant exercise of candor, peer-to-peer accountability, seeking proactive collaboration, and the broadest inclusion that you find embedded in the culture of highest-performing teams. For example, Raman describes the approach to team-ship and the importance of candor within their team at P&G: "There were two constructs we lived by: one was *It's more important to get the results than to be right*. The second was *High conflict, high respect for a functional family*." It echoes what we heard from Bill Connors and Bob Pittman in chapter 3. "Our insight was that worrying about egos or pride in a meeting is a terrible waste of focus. So, it became known that individuals don't win or lose in meetings; winning or losing was only measured in the market outcomes, not in our debates. So, it's better to have a tough meeting which translates to winning in the market, rather than a nice meeting, which makes people feel good about themselves." But individual contribution was crucial, so much so that they created a personal accountability grid and shared it transparently. The grid went so far as to display people's faces and names against their quarterly commitments. Every quarter when the whole team met, people stood up with the grid to explain the results, whether good or bad. "Initially, some were really worried about this construct, because they imagined people's faces and names against things, and they were worried about how they would feel if their photo was associated with failure in a quarter," says Raman. "But it ended up being a strong driver not to have such poor performance, and overall it was one of the most sought-after things among members of the team who wanted to have clearer clarity and accountability for themselves, and a way to be celebrated for their winning. People used to walk up and say, '*How do I get my face up on that chart? And what am I going to be held accountable for and I want to stand up and explain what I learned in the process.*' It became a positive driver of personal accountability and team cohesion and success."

MIGUEL MILANO: CRACKING THE CO-ELEVATION CODE

In sales, many might expect to find a high degree of internal competition or self-interested behaviors. Yet, at one of the most successful sales organizations, Miguel Milano has called on the power of teamship and Co-elevation behaviors. Milano is the president and chief revenue officer at Salesforce and leads the company's global sales team. But when it comes to some of the most precious areas to sales leaders, setting sales quotas and deciding who in their team will take the limited number of promotions to VP, for example, his senior leaders are called on to co-create in order to reach the decision rather than lobby upward for their piece of the pie. "I believe a lot in leadership and I believe more in teams—I expect a great deal from my team and they don't let each other down," says Milano. With sales quotas, Milano will propose an overall target, then ask his senior leaders to settle on their final figures. "I say to the team that I leave it with you to decide if anyone can take more or less and help each other out," says Milano. "Two weeks later, my chief operating officer tells me what they have agreed to do. I trust my team. I want them to feel that this has been a joint decision."

The alternative to asking the sales leads to collaborate on their quotas is individual negotiation. Milano says, "It's more efficient for sales leaders to work out quotas against a shared goal because they're closest to the deals." Revenues were up 11 percent to $34.9 billion in Salesforce's fiscal year 2024 in what Chair and CEO Marc Benioff described as "a phenomenal year of transformation." Milano's answer to sales growth at Salesforce is Co-elevating behaviors and teamship. In addition to relying on teamship for such important negotiations, the teams also stress-test their annual plans with each other. That process, full of calling out challenges and contributing innovations, might normally fall on defensiveness, but not among a Co-elevating sales team committed to each other's success.

REVATHI ADVAITHI: THE EMOTIONAL RESONANCE OF CO-ELEVATION IN PRACTICE

When Revathi Advaithi joined Flex as CEO in 2019, she didn't just bring a change of strategy—she brought new thinking about what it is to be a leader of teams in today's volatile business environment. Advaithi was a first-time CEO, the first female CEO at that $26 billion design and manufacturing company, and a woman of color stepping into a highly visible Fortune 500 leadership position in a historically male-dominated industry. The strategic goal was to position Flex, founded in Silicon Valley in 1969, as the most trusted global technology, supply chain, and manufacturing solutions partner to improve the world. Advaithi says, "When many people think of manufacturing, they think of the Industrial Revolution and manual factory lines. It was crucial that Flex rolled out a new strategy that spoke to our position at the forefront of manufacturing innovation and growth."

At the heart of Advaithi's new approach to the business was a new social contract of deep mutual respect, open sharing that delivered deep personal care, peers honoring commitments to each other and holding each other accountable, and a culture of constant learning and adapting—all echoes of the Co-elevation behaviors and processes of teamship. And when Advaithi talks about teams, you will be struck by the power of a deep emotional commitment to the humanity of teamship. She describes purposeful bonding as a way of building the personal trust and relationships that powers peer-to-peer accountability and collaboration. It's the foundation of the 10 shifts. Advaithi explains: "My way of connecting with my teams is simple. I like to get to know them as people, not just as work colleagues. Who are they? What do they enjoy doing? What's their life like? What are their values? I tend to spend time getting to know my teams. I invite them to my home, go out for dinners, see how they interact with each other, etc. So, with time, we build trust and respect for each other. This doesn't happen overnight. On this foundation my teams are able to align with each other before feeling compelled to come to me for decisions. This contract among them leads to the team increasing their communication with each other, coming from a place of curiosity rather than ego, helping us to connect as a leadership team and to reinforce that we all shared the same goal—transforming Flex for the better."

Today you will see Flex described as "one of the world's most critical manufacturing companies" by *Fortune*, and you will find the business behind charging stations for electric vehicles, in wearable injectors to improve dose accuracy for patients receiving healthcare, at work on 5G connectivity systems, and helping other global organizations design and manufacture domestic appliances.

AGILE TEAMS ARE ALIGNED TEAMS

Members of world-class teams know what their teammates are working on, what goals are being activated; they know everyone is aligned on the same critical mission. It's a promise of teams successfully adopting agile as their operating system. They have achieved what few teams have: clear alignment to a single North Star and also agreement on the trade-offs needed among them to get there, because transparency and inclusion are built into their collaborative process. Some managers during the pandemic who had to adjust to having virtual associates on their team would often ask, "How do I know if my people are working and are they being fully productive?" The answer is simple. If you don't know what they are working on and if they are being productive, then you have not done your job of having clear sprints of outcome-oriented work aligned within the team. What's missing is the power and importance of agile as the new operating system for that team. Like the P&G team's accountability grid and regular open debates on each critical business area, regular Stress Testing at the end of agile sprints brings full team visibility to all the necessary trade-offs. It's similar to what the Salesforce sales organization and Flex teams do for each other. Once committed to full alignment and the transparency of conflicts and interdependencies, achieving the team's goals and vision is within reach of any team. What does that do for leaders? It allows them to free up time, to look more outwardly, to engage key constituencies, and to ensure that the most important strategic questions are brought to the team to discuss. This does not mean that the leader becomes the sole arbiter of strategy either. Instead they use regular monthly transformation meetings with prior asynchronous input, broadly asking,

➤ "What opportunities are we missing as a business?"
➤ "What risks are we not paying enough attention to?"

As we discussed in chapter 7, this assures that foresight (and teamship practices like the Foresight Five Minutes) is brought to the business organically, meaning new strategies and directions that we couldn't even possibly imagine before will become a reality of the new teamship operating system. And again, by adopting an agile framework with transparent and inclusive engagement across teams, it also allows us to leave our teams to their work feeling engaged, empowered, and resilient. But few leaders have that peace of mind; most teams are not that aligned, or if they think they are aligned it's only at the top level of a shared mission, not as they double-click down into the priorities and trade-offs. Embracing Stress Testing and Collaborative Problem-Solving at the broadest levels of the organization is critical to alignment; practices that help team members share openly where they are struggling help everyone align where trade-offs and resources are needed. Alignment at all levels naturally flows from the regular adoption of teamship practices in this book.

TEAMSHIP PRACTICES

Aside from all the teamship practices that preceded this chapter, one new teamship practice fuels the shift from silos to alignment:

> ➤ **Alignment Collaborative Problem-Solving:** This teamship practice helps to both identify areas of misalignment and then resolve them using the CPS method we encountered in chapter 6.

The Alignment Diagnostic

STEP ONE: *Team Discussion About Alignment*

By Co-elevating, co-creating, adopting process changes, working in agile sprints, and leveraging new tools and embracing AI, the outcome of the previous nine shifts will lead us toward becoming a constantly aligned organization. We should have broken down silos and headed off narrow-minded competition for resources, because the transparency and co-creation bring shared ownership and a greater focus on enterprise winning. It is worth reflecting on the great teams we encountered in the early chapters of the book: Bill Connors's at Xfinity, or Bob Pittman's at iHeart. They all thrived by collaborating and creating value from their interdependencies. These teams were engaged, transparent, and candid about the trade-offs they needed to make as they aligned toward their shared North Star. That's what's missing in most teams: the level of commitment to agility and then candor, peer-to-peer accountability, collaboration, and Co-elevation that we see in the P&G team's work. But what is also clear from the P&G team is that alignment is not a one-and-done exercise. We need an alignment high-return practice that can be used periodically. Alignment to a North Star needs to be sustained in constant agile sprints.

STEP TWO: *Diagnostic Questions*

All team members give a score of 1 to 5 for the following questions (1: Strongly disagree, 2: Disagree, 3: Neutral, 4: Agree, 5: Strongly agree):

- All team members are aligned and committed to a shared mission that acts as the team's North Star and the priorities and trade-offs we are making to get there.
- This team strives for transformation and innovation rather than maintaining the status quo and running "business as usual."
- I truly enjoy being a part of this team.
- This is a winning team that consistently meets or exceeds its goals.
- We are achieving our full potential as a team.

The diagnostic must be administered by a team member who is seen as agnostic and trusted, as the scoring is private and will not be attributed to individuals. Use an online survey tool or the Diagnostic Assessment on my website.

Red Flag Rule and Red Flag Replays

The Red Flag Rule for team behavior for shifting from silos to alignment is: "We are aligned on the North Star and the priorities and trade-offs to get there." Calling for a Red Flag Replay on this particular shift within a month of practicing the below teamship practices and then regularly thereafter is an opportunity to hold space to talk about where things may have gone off the rails, to check that our new behavioral commitments are being observed and teamship practices are being implemented.

Teamship Practice: Alignment CPS

We will use the Collaborative Problem-Solving teamship practice we encountered in chapter 6. Each numbered point below is a single CPS exercise focusing on fundamental questions about the North Star that would give our teams a powerful start toward alignment. Use these to elicit reflection from your team. As we learned in chapter 6, it's most beneficial to gather initial thoughts on these asynchronously and then utilize a meeting to reach a decision.

1. **What is our ultimate mission and what will our world and our customers' world look like when we get there?** Using a question like this can quickly show the lack of clarity and alignment around the mission but can also be used to triangulate good suggestions among the team. Share all the asynchronous answers in advance and use small breakout groups to refine those into a set of options for a smaller group to take offline and bring to a conclusion. Let there be one more round of Stress Testing with the new mission, or perhaps a Decision Board with key questions you want to gain insight on from the team.

2. **What are the three most remarkable things that will be present when we are truly on our way to achieving our mission that are not present now?**

3. **What are the biggest items to attack, or the biggest hills we must take to achieve our North Star?** We then need to assign and do a CPS process for each of the agreed-upon big hills followed by regular ongoing Stress Testing of the hill owner's progress at the end of regular agile sprints.

4. **What blockers are most likely to derail us that we need to fortify around? And what are the suggestions to address each?** A great process to unearth these blockers and find the solutions for each is a Decision Board (see chapter 6).

The point is that the CPS process and regular Stress Testing should be used iteratively to go more and more granularly down to a level of shared insight and alignment among the broadest relevant team members. I believe great untapped wisdom exists in our ability to Team Out inside and outside our organizations. It starts with a curiosity and growth mindset and then carries on by leveraging the teamship practices for more expansive engagement. Our teams need to gather the collective data, analyze it as a team, and come to bold decisions. Perhaps we just need practice with a coach, but ultimately the responsibility comes back to the team to be each other's coaches. Teamship is a new set of muscles we need to learn to exercise. As you will find each time you carry out the Alignment CPS, you will create a list of other misaligned or innovative topics to cover in future sessions.

JOIN THE MOVEMENT

This book is a call for a movement. It's a call for a radical shift in our traditional thinking of leadership, and an awakening of the power of teamship that has gone undercurated, against decades of putting leaders alone in the spotlight. It's an awakening to maximize the value from interdependency co-created and brought to life in prior chapters. The simple invitation is just to start this journey. As any team member, you can pose the recontracting discussions and open up an awareness among your team for shifts you all want to make. I always say, after beginning this process, you don't expect perfection, you just expect people to awaken to hope and possibility, and then we go on a journey to creating a higher degree of candor and opening up more personal risk-taking among us. This is a social contract of candor in service of each other, not punitive or cutting each other down. This is why we also purposefully build greater relationships with our peers in order to continue to fortify and uplift the courage that we need to be candid and to hold each other accountable.

To practice that candor and accountability, we begin with feedback around ideas, then we open up the aperture to others with Collaborative Problem-Solving in the most robust and inclusive ways, leveraging the cutting-edge, collaborative tools and AI that are available to us to Team Out in a modern world. Also, as we launch new initiatives out of these innovative ideas and move toward execution, we dig into Stress Testing at the end of critical agile sprints, where we once again invite a broader, more inclusive group of individuals into the collaborative process, assuring we minimize risks and gain greater foresight, looking around corners, and finding additional innovations from the broadest team. All of this brings the kind of constant alignment in an iterative, agile process that isn't one-and-done. This is a constant practice of using these tools to awaken, to expand and gain broader and bolder insight, broader and bolder innovation that yields the kind of outcomes that are disruptive and exponential. This is what Sundar Raman does. This is what Miguel Milano does. This is what Revathi Advaithi does and what Tarang Amin and Bill Connors and Patti Poppe and all the other great teamship leaders in this book do. And this is what we invite you to start doing.

We also invite you to share your stories with me on LinkedIn. Share your story of your execution of this work and we'll invite you into a growing community of people who are learning from each other. The world needs a movement of people committed to supporting and coaching each other—teammates committed to coaching and being coached—bringing your peers to a new way of working. I've also consistently seen those who adopt these new practices in the workplace report a change in their personal lives as elevating their relationships with their families. And by Teaming Out, and expanding these practices into the world, and bringing a new way of collaborating, a new set of teamship processes and tools, a new set of Co-elevating behaviors, a new way of engaging, the world will be better for it.

AFTERWORD

How you use the book is flexible; it's up to you and your team.

I suggest the book be read in one go by the team, and then the execution among the team may be done in short teamship adoption sprints with what I call regular transformation meetings. Once everyone reads the book, make a commitment among the team to introduce and discuss each shift and adopt the teamship practices, chapter by chapter, every two weeks or perhaps every month. It could be helpful if one member of the team or an outside facilitator coach supports this early adoption. It can be any member of the team committed to the process or you can certainly reach out to my organization for support. We have a process that does not just follow the chapters, but this book was designed to work for you in that self-administered way.

In the first transformation meeting, you discuss chapters

2 and 3 and take the diagnostic for those two chapters and begin to apply the teamship practices from chapter 3.

Then in the next transformation meeting 2–4 weeks later you do a Red Flag Replay for your first teamship sprint on candor. In that second transformation meeting you do the discussion and diagnostic for the fourth chapter on purposeful bonding and begin to practice the bonding teamship practices.

You carry on this way till all the shifts and teamship practices are being discussed, diagnosed, and experienced.

Ongoing, as a team, look at all the Red Flag Rules and do a Red Flag Replay and take the entire diagnostic at once. This would be a regular process every quarter or six months.

ACKNOWLEDGMENTS

The most important acknowledgment is to my coauthor, Paul Hill, who joined this team more than five years ago for what seemed to be a one-year documentation of twenty years of research. His patience and his Co-elevating and co-creating abilities over the last five years of this project have made this book possible. I also want to thank his wife, Sabelline. There is an extraordinary untold story of how her support and commitment to getting the book done helped get us to the finish line. I am eternally grateful.

This book exists thanks to the generous insight of leaders, change agents, and entrepreneurs who have shared their passion to elevate teams and change the world. They include Michael Ackerbauer, Revathi Advaithi, Tarang Amin, Pedro Carrilho, Carol Clements, Bill Connors, Mandy Fields, George Fisher, Jason Green, Drew Houston, Fran Katsoudas, Arvind Krishna, Nickle LaMoreaux, Enrique Lores, Kory Marchisotto, Juan Martin, Miguel Milano, Matt Mullenweg,

Bob Pittman, Monica Pool Knox, Patti Poppe, Kerry Preston, Sundar Raman, Chuck Robbins, Rachel Romer, Khalil Smith, Eric Starkloff, Rob Thomas, and Sergey Young. Their vision and commitment has helped to shape each chapter and we are deeply grateful.

There are dozens of amazing people we spoke to who shared their thoughts and ideas at different stages of our journey whose names do not feature in the book, but whose thinking left its mark. They include Frank Blake, Bechara Choucair, Brian Cornell, Lori Digulla, Fama Francisco, Thomas Kurian, Eileen Mahoney, Darren Murph, Mark Reuss, Alexi Robichaux, Dan Schulman, Dan Shapiro, Nick Sonnenberg, Astro Teller, and Gil West.

I'd also like to thank dear friends of mine, Jeff and Beth Mori, who have been lifelong Co-elevating friends and role models in their relationship.

I want to thank Jack, Jacobo, Michael, Tim, and Shadi for being living embodiments of Co-elevation.

Thanks, Mom, for growing with me throughout life.

To Peter Diamandis for always being there.

FROM PAUL

Thanks to my wise and wonderful wife, Sabelline, and my four kids for their love and support through lost weekends. Dana Zelicha introduced me to mindfulness and changed my life while I was writing this book; there aren't enough words of gratitude. Three people Keith introduced me to have become amazing mentors: Susan Sobbott, Kay Walker, and John Galvin. Thank you for your counsel and friendship.

FROM KEITH AND PAUL

As ever, special thanks are due to our literary agent, Esmond Harmsworth, who delivers compass point advice and ideas when the path seems uncertain. Thanks to Hollis Heimbouch and her team at HarperCollins for all of their expertise and support, particularly our editor, Kirby Sandmeyer, for her commitment to excellence and asking razor-sharp questions on readers' behalf.

Cody Thompson brought searching questions and research insight to the early stages of the project. Cody, your work proved invaluable to the very end, thank you.

We would like to thank the many brilliant people who critiqued the manuscript and gave valuable comments that helped us shape the final draft. Many thanks for the kind contributions of: Sandeep Angra, Sean Behr, Justin Choi (who came up with the title *Never Lead Alone*—amazing, thank you), Suketu Gandhi, David Kidder, Sandeep Kulkarni, Pat St. Laurent, Alan May, Shadi May, Kim Richards (who first mentioned teamship to me years ago), Len Schlesinger, Eivind Slaaen, Christie Smith, and Matt Walter.

To everyone at Ferrazzi Greenlight! . . . Jim Hannon, who has been on this journey from the start. Don't know where

ACKNOWLEDGMENTS

I would be without your support. Thank you, Diane Brown, Harris Fanaroff, Mike Hernandez, LadyAnn Juan, Hector Luna, Gavin McKay, J.J. Mechoso, Clair Nanadiego, Ronen Olshansky, Kaitlyn Parent, Darren Reinke, Josh Sabino, Mary Schnitker, Kimberly Stewart, and Morgan Williams.

APPENDIX:
RED FLAG RULES AND DIAGNOSTIC
QUESTIONS FOR EACH SHIFT

CHAPTER 2: Shifting from Hub-and-Spoke to
the Leader to Co-Elevation of the Team

Red Flag Rule:

*We are equally committed to all goals of the team and each
other to get there.*

CHAPTER 3: Shifting from Conflict
Avoidance to Candor

Red Flag Rule:

We speak courageously.

Diagnostic Questions:

➤ All team members are willing to directly challenge one
another, even when it is risky to do so, or the topic is
outside their "swim lane" or area of expertise.

➤ All team members actively hold each other
accountable for one another's commitments and
outcomes.

CHAPTER 4: Shifting from Serendipitous Relationships to Purposeful Team Bond-Building

Red Flag Rule:
We are truly committed to one another.

Diagnostic Questions:

➤ All team members respect and value what every other member of this team contributes.

➤ All team members have established caring, trusting, and supportive relationships with all other members of this team.

➤ All team members proactively deepen and improve their relationships with the network of those critical to our success and turn associates important to the team into real advocates.

CHAPTER 5: Shifting from Individual to Team Resilience

Red Flag Rule:
We lift each other up.

Diagnostic Question:

➤ All team members feel responsible to lift each other's energy.

CHAPTER 6: Shifting to Elevate Collaboration: Broader and Bolder Co-Creation Through Meeting Shifting

Red Flag Rule:
We co-create broadly to innovate boldly.

Red Flag Rule:
We leverage technology to elevate our collaboration.

Diagnostic Questions:
➤ This team creates significant, tangible value from the interdependencies that exist between us.
➤ We are not impeded by hierarchy or a reliance on positional authority.
➤ This team crosses the finish line together, and we do whatever it takes to deliver on every aspect of the team's collective performance.
➤ All team members follow through on their own individual commitments and hold themselves accountable for their outcomes.
➤ Meetings are welcome and productive because we use them sparingly and as a complement with the most modern collaborative and AI tools that save us time and allow us to engage inclusively.
➤ We are inclusive and invite the broadest diverse set of opinions to find the most innovative solutions.

CHAPTER 7: Shifting to Agile as the New Operating System for Your Team

---

Red Flag Rule:
Agile is our operating system.

Diagnostic Question:
➤ We adopt agile principles in our work process and iteratively prioritize and adapt to new information and competing demands.

CHAPTER 8: Shifting from a Culture of Scarce Praise to Peer Celebration and Recognition

Red Flag Rule:
We celebrate each other.

Diagnostic Question:
➤ All team members encourage and celebrate one another's success.

CHAPTER 9: Shifting to Diversity, Inclusion, and Belonging

Red Flag Rule:
We believe a diversity of people and voices achieves breakthrough performance.

CHAPTER 10: Shifting to a Team of Seekers Who Are Each Other's Coaches

Red Flag Rule:
We coach each other.

Diagnostic Questions:
➤ Are we a team of seekers? All team members are aware of and open about their areas of growth and actively pursuing corrective development.
➤ Are we each other's coaches? All team members are personally invested in one another's development and are proactively providing peer-to-peer coaching on their teammates' hard and soft skills and competencies.

CHAPTER 11: Shifting from Silos to Alignment

Red Flag Rule:
We are aligned on the North Star and the priorities and trade-offs to get there.

Diagnostic Questions:
- ➤ All team members are aligned and committed to a shared mission that acts as the team's North Star and the priorities and trade-offs we are making to get there.
- ➤ This team strives for transformation and innovation rather than maintaining the status quo and running "business as usual."
- ➤ I truly enjoy being a part of this team.
- ➤ This is a winning team that consistently meets or exceeds its goals.
- ➤ We are achieving our full potential as a team.

NOTES

Chapter 1: Cracking the Code of Teamship

17 It's true: I first came across this phrase being used in Alcoholics Anonymous programs during research for my book *Who's Got Your Back*.

Chapter 3: Shifting from Conflict Avoidance to Candor

41 on my website: https://ferrazzigreenlight.com/high-impact-team-assessment-questionnaire/.

51 says Dalio: Ray Dalio, "Work Principle: Show Candidates Your Warts," n.d., accessed February 24, 2024, https://www.principles.com/principles/af0ca990-6eb9-45cd-bf07-b12580fafafa/.

Chapter 4: Shifting From Serendipitous Relationships to Purposeful Team Bond-Building

62 on my website: https://ferrazzigreenlight.com/high-impact-team-assessment-questionnaire/.

69 in Northern California: Ivan Penn, "PG&E Ordered to Pay $3.5 Million Fine for Causing Deadly Fire," *New York Times*, June 18, 2020, https://www.nytimes.com/2020/06/18/business/energy-environment/pge-camp-fire-sentenced.html

Chapter 5: Shifting from Individual to Team Resilience

76 another 60 percent: D. Codella, "World Mental Health Day Highlights the Need for Mental Health Support," *BetterUp Blog*, 2022, accessed March 25, 2024, https://www.betterup.com/blog/mental-health-support-needs.

76 lower absenteeism: "National Safety Council and NORC at the University of Chicago Announce New Mental Health Cost

Calculator to Demonstrate Why Investing in Mental Health Is Good for Business," NORC, 2021, accessed March 25, 2024, https://www.norc.org/research/library/national-safety-council -and-norc-at-the-university-of-chicago-an.html.

78 on my website: https://ferrazzigreenlight.com/high-impact-team -assessment-questionnaire/.

83 *Health & Well-Being*: U.S. Surgeon General's Framework for Workplace Mental Health & Well-Being 2022, https://www.hhs .gov/sites/default/files/workplace-mental-health-well-being.pdf.

Chapter 6: Shifting to Elevate Collaboration: Broader and Bolder Co-Creation Through Meeting Shifting

104 on my website: https://ferrazzigreenlight.com/high-impact-team -assessment-questionnaire/.

115 meetings is unnecessary: Otter.ai and Dr. Steven G. Rogelberg, "The Cost of Unnecessary Meeting Attendance," September 26, 2022, https://public.otter.ai/reports/The_Cost_of_Unnecessary _Meeting_Attendance.pdf.

116 "making a decision": O. R. Royle, "Shopify's CFO Explains How Its New Meeting Cost Calculator Works, and How It Will Cut 474,000 Events in 2023: 'Time Is Money,'" *Fortune*, July 13, 2023, accessed March 25, 2024, https://fortune.com/2023/07/13 /shopify-meeting-cost-calculator-expert-warning/.

Chapter 7: Shifting to Agile as the New Operating System for Your Team

122 strategic change programs: R. Carucci, "Executives Fail to Execute Strategy Because They're Too Internally Focused," *Harvard Business Review*, July 2017, accessed March 25, 2024, https://hbr .org/2017/11/executives-fail-to-execute-strategy-because-theyre -too-internally-focused.

127 on my website: https://ferrazzigreenlight.com/high-impact-team -assessment-questionnaire/.

128 "the highest priority": K. Beck, M. Beedle, et al., "Principles Behind the Agile Manifesto," 2001, accessed March 25, 2024, https://agilemanifesto.org/principles.html.

Chapter 8: Shifting from a Culture of Scarce Praise to Peer Celebration and Recognition

144 on my website: https://ferrazzigreenlight.com/high-impact-team -assessment-questionnaire/.

149 Oprah Winfrey once said: Harvard University Commencement Address, 2013.

Chapter 10: Shifting to a Team of Seekers Who Are Each Other's Coaches

173 on my website: https://ferrazzigreenlight.com/high-impact-team-assessment-questionnaire/.

177 others perceive us: S. Edinger, "You Are Not the Best Judge of You," *Harvard Business Review*, November 2011, accessed March 25, 2024, https://hbr.org/2011/11/you-are-not-the-best-judge-of.

180 5/5/5 formats: S. D. Friedman, "How to Get Your Team to Coach Each Other," *Harvard Business Review*, March 2015, accessed March 25, 2024, https://hbr.org/2015/03/how-to-get-your-team-to-coach-each-other.

Chapter 11: Shifting from Silos to Alignment

186 "year of transformation": "Salesforce Announces Strong Fourth Quarter and Fiscal 2024 Results," Salesforce, news release, March 31, 2024, accessed March 31, 2024, https://investor.salesforce.com/press-releases/press-release-details/2024/Salesforce-Announces-Strong-Fourth-Quarter-Fiscal-2024-Results/default.aspx.

188 manufacture domestic appliances: "Most Powerful Women 2022: Revathi Advaithi," *Fortune*, October 11, 2022, accessed March 31, 2024, https://fortune.com/ranking/most-powerful-women/2022/revathi-advaithi/.

192 on my website: https://ferrazzigreenlight.com/high-impact-team-assessment-questionnaire/.

ABOUT THE AUTHORS

KEITH FERRAZZI is a #1 *New York Times* bestselling author of *Never Eat Alone, Who's Got Your Back, Leading Without Authority,* and *Competing in the New World of Work*. An accomplished speaker, entrepreneur, and investor, Keith is recognized as the world's top executive team coach, having coached the transformation of Fortune 50 corporations, the World Bank, Unicorns, and governments. You've perhaps read his columns in *Harvard Business Review, Forbes,* the *Wall Street Journal, Fortune, Fast Company,* and *Inc. Magazine*. Former CMO and head of sales at Deloitte and Starwood Hotels, Keith founded Ferrazzi Greenlight—a team coaching firm—and leads the Greenlight Research Institute focused on team transformation.

PAUL HILL is an award-winning business editor and crime correspondent turned editorial consultant. He has written—and ghostwritten—work for some of the world's most respected publications, and he crafts nonfiction books and thought-provoking articles for global business leaders. He lives in the UK.

Keith Ferrazzi

The world's best teams don't win solely because of leadership; they win largely because of their teamship. Now that you have the tools and practices to ignite your teamship journey, what is your vision for success in the next 6-12 months?

Learn how Ferrazzi's teamship services can support your team and access complementary resources by scanning below:

Speaking | Workshops | Team Coaching | Virtual Learning

Speaking:
- A 60-minute keynote to challenge and inspire your organization to think differently about how they manage teams for greater innovation, alignment, and Co-elevation®.

Workshops:
- 1- to 2-day immersive workshops for leaders who will spearhead the teamship transformation in your organization, conducted through training, breakout groups and facilitated coaching.
- Co-created organizational rollout and communication plan for lasting impact.

Team Coaching:
- Significantly shift the team's ways of working, activate Co-elevation® behaviors, and break down silos to enhance collaboration and innovative thinking.
- This high-touch, custom approach involves team coaching, peer-to-peer coaching, and skilled facilitation across a 6- to 12-month period of virtual and in-person sessions for sustained adoption.

Virtual Learning:
- Access the diagnostic survey, training videos, and templates/instructions for teamship practices.
- Simple guides and presentations to make it easy for team leaders to facilitate sessions, scaling the journey through limitless teams.

Keith's research can be found in prestigious publications, including *Harvard Business Review*, *Forbes*, the *Wall Street Journal*, *Fortune*, *Fast Company*, and *Inc. Magazine*, where his columns serve as valuable insights for business leaders.

www.keithferrazzi.com